Asteroids in Astrology 1

Centaurs, Damocloids & Scattered Disc Objects
Series: Asteroids in Astrology 1
Author: Benjamin Adamah

Lay-out: Sylvia Carrilho, www.burokd.nl
Editor: Orenda Bol

ISBN 978-94-92355-40-9

Publisher:

VAMzzz Publishing
P.O. Box 3340
1001 AC Amsterdam
The Netherlands
www.vamzzz.com
contactvamzzz@gmail.com

ASTEROIDS IN ASTROLOGY 1

CENTAURS DAMOCLOIDS

SCATTERED DISC OBJECTS

Benjamin Adamah

VAMzzz PUBLISHING

CONTENTS

LIST OF IMAGES

V Cusp 4 ☌ Cardi
2003 WC7 / 1999 TB
ELATUS
5 ♉ 12
☌ Niobe
Georges Bedau
Elatus ☌ Saturnus
1999 TB
29 ♍
△ Rhada
☿ Pholus ✶ ☾
Pan 2002 PN34 △ ⚷
♒
Utopia
Cusp 6 ☌ Nessus
Pallas ♌
□ Hidalgo □ ♀
□
♍
☉ 5 ♍ 22 ☌ Siva
Chiron / Ixion
12 ☌ Chrisodan
Nessus
△
Tamminarsh
△ ☌ ♀ Ariadne
Rousseau
Hidalgo
Echeclus
Bannu
☾ ♋ 6°00
Schadow 6 ♯ ρ
Salacia
Villa
♍
2 △ Rockefellia
Ocas
verdeling
☾ ☌ 2001 XA 255
✶ 1988 XB
♍
Lovejoy | Schadow
Salacia
vreemde seksuele afwijkingen
Ho 12
2002
Perfectiosdi
uitdrukkelijk
Sura.
ORIO
△ Hylonome
✶ Bienor
Amycodaea
♀
♀
2002 PN34
Juno / ♇ / Dardura / pandora
☌ ☾
Bahrest
♍
veroordeling negers
seksuele vergrijpen / afwijk
seksueel gedrag
△ Ascendant 29 ♋
Sedna human
☿ ☌ Varda ↔ chaos
Verdun
Sethras
pholus
amun
□ Φ
29 ♍
Carinerva
VATT Veder
P ☌
△ ♌
Tuhmet
ERIS ☌ M
Nessus ☌ 12
△
↔ ☌ Deima
10
△ Alamannia / CXBI / Vircheru Nako
chaos

INTRODUCTION

Asteroid astrology is booming, especially among the younger generation of astrology students and the more open minded professionals. The point is that the additional use of asteroids in a personal chart, or even in mundane astrology, is like putting on reading glasses in a dimly lit room. All of a sudden everything becomes so much lighter and clearer than before! And what an expansion of your horizon apart from this much more detailed picture that emerges out of the blur you used to work with. I mean, just take two simple asteroids as an example: How can you really define what a client will be most *passionate about,* without including Eros? How can you tell a client *what kind of partner would be most suitable* without analyzing his or her Juno – apart from basic routines like analyzing the 7th house, its ruler etc.? Is passion not a major thing in anyone's life? Is an unfulfilled desire for the ideal partner and soul mate not a motive for people to blow their brains out ever since the invention of gunpowder? Asteroid astrology is not *"just a little extra"*.

I'm 55 years old while writing these lines, and yes, I started old school with the "classic ten" (Sun up to and including Pluto) and without a computer, doing my calculations with boring algorithm-tables and an ephemerides-collection the size of Shanghai's telephone directory. I did not even use the Black Moons in those days, which I cannot possibly imagine now or even ten years ago. Luckily, today we are blessed with amazing computer-software that enables us astrologers to do our research roughly a thousand times faster than was possible twenty-five years ago. And then there are these fantastic websites, like serennu.com, where you can test tens of thousands of different asteroids. Not all of them are very useful, thank God, but many of them are (at least a 1000) and they fill up the missing links in an amazing way! Some asteroid emancipation has been going on so far and adding Chiron, Juno, Pallas, Vesta and Ceres already makes a difference. But once this new astrological dimension has opened up to you full scope, sticking to just these five extras is like sticking to the same five movies on Netflix each year while having the full range of hundreds of newly added movies at your disposal.

However, a huge rift has formed between our technical possibilities – focused on extended chart calculation – and the information needed to read those juicy asteroids-including charts! Very few books on asteroids were published this far and much information is vague, outdated, incomplete, just one line, useless spiritual fantasy and/or hopelessly scattered online. And on this base you have to become an insider first, before you can discriminate the serious asteroid material from the rubbish. A sort of impossible paradox. This problem had annoyed me for many years, until I finally took up the idea to personally categorize what were – in my opinion – the most useful astrological data on asteroids in astrology. This resulted in developing and testing a reliable system for extracting their significance in a chart as there were many different interpretations of the same asteroid, if there was any information on the asteroid at all. A few brave and skilled online pioneers, who published some more useful material on the subject out of the same need that I had, was inspiring, but, especially as the Dutch astrological tradition leans heavily on "psychological cosmic mining" I had to follow my own course. While checking the validity of available material of the moment, I used the discovery-charts, the *memes* attached to asteroid-names (when they had one) and the testing of my hypotheses as a foundation for my final conclusions about asteroid A, asteroid B, etc. Hylonome, for example, has a wagon-load of internet cut & paste clutter attached to it, that spreads a substantially wrong interpretation.

Distilling the true significance of asteroids, beyond the simple forensic use (which is mainly a "Main-belt thing") is a painstaking and long process and in the case of Hylonome (and Bienor) I even used 150 test horoscopes. What turned out to be of crucial importance was the use of extremely small orbs for asteroid-aspects and paying special attention to conjunctions and oppositions. Something I would advise to every other asteroid researcher!

In 2016 – 2017 my asteroid obsession resulted in a bulky 671-page book, written in Dutch, titled ASTEROÏDEN-GIDS (Asteroid Guide). Based on 750,000 pages of research-data it describes the astrological meaning and significance of 950 asteroids, classified in 16 astronomical categories. These categories are:

- Aten asteroids
- Apollo asteroids
- Hungary-asteroids
- Amor asteroid
- Main-belt asteroids
- Cybele asteroids
- Hilda asteroids
- Trojans
- Plutinos
- Cubewanos
- Haumeids
- Special Neptune-resonants
- Centaurs
- SDOs and Detached Objects
- Damocloids
- Ex(Comets)

Because a proper English translation of this Shanghai's telephone directory-sized asteroid-guide does take some time, I decided to divide the book into six parts and publish them separately.

So you are now reading the first volume of an updated series. The translations will have extras, like added new asteroids; in this volume: *Dziewanna, G!kún'hòmdímà, 2007 TG422, Kondojiro, Zhulong* and *Ka'epaoka'awela* or *Bee-Zed*, as well as recently released official names like *Aphidas and Gonggong* (formerly unofficial name: Snow white) which are not included in the 2017 Dutch edition. They will be presented in clear-cut sections, which, like in this first volume, combines four categories of asteroids which overlap in terms of equal features.

GENERAL CHARACTERISTICS

This brings us to some of the general characteristics of Centaurs, Damocloids, Scattered Disc Objects (SDOs) – including Detached Objects or E-SDOs – and ex(Comets). What are they? Or to expand the question: *are* there, in general, significant features, typically only for one special class of asteroids? To answer this last question: yes and no.

Yes, because astronomers classified asteroids into categories, mostly based on the resonance their orbits have or do not have with a certain planet. Many objects for example have a "click" with Jupiter (Main-belt asteroids) or Neptune (Plutinos). Making the shift to astrology and studying their influence in charts, indeed provides us with certain group-features.

No, because there are too many exceptions to the rule, like objects in the Main-belt with the depth and complexity of Haumeids or Centaurs or, contrarily, far away objects with features that are not very clear or illuminating, but just explicit or annoying, when their extremely slow passing transits temporary mess up your life. Some objects are really into the depth-psychology stuff, whilst others are pretty one-dimensional, just like there are really simple and very complex people, despite the fact that everyone has a complex birth chart.

CENTAURS

Back to the asteroids who come to the fore in the first volume of this series. Let's start with the Centaurs. Chiron was already standard included in every astro-software package for a decade or two. No professional astrologer wants to skip the "wound in the client's soul", his or her "blind spots" or "second midlife crises" aka reality-check around Chiron's return (at about the age of 51). To those who like to keep it simple this may be a disappointing message, but despite Chiron being an important player in a chart, many other Centaurs are at least as interesting. Nessus, Pylenor, Hylonome, Bienor, Crantor, Thereus, Asbolus – once you get to know them, you can't do without them anymore. Doing financial astrology without using 1998 BU48 and 2001 BL41 will be a bit amateurish. And then there is this parasite 2002 PN34, and the noisy but often correct "whistle blower on fake news" 2001 KF77 (Alex Jones' natal chart is really stuffed with this object). To make it even more spicy: Centaur 2000 CO104 is pretty specific about orgasm. You cannot do a proper sexual astrological analysis without 2000 CO104.

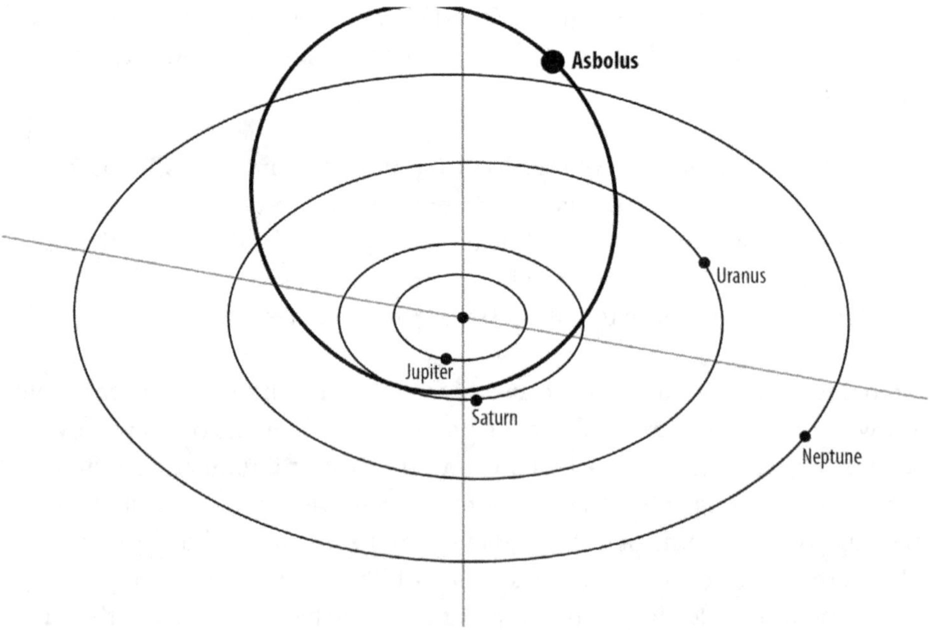

Orbit of Asbolus

Like Jupiter-Trojans, Centaurs are dramatic entities. However, there are also big differences. In the case of Jupiter-Trojans the drama is rooted in most cases in intrinsically unbalanced yang-energy, leading to excesses or at least the potential for it and the socially enforced smothering of ones powers. Centaurs are more complex. They are authentic anarchists, they do not shun the fringes of society and most of them are full of pretty schizophrenic psychological contrasts and/or ambitions. Hence there is a longing for a psycho-synthetic healing i.e. a homeostasis, wherein these bipolar features coincide in one amazing, synergistic power. And, once this is accomplished, an impressive creativity and/or originality can come to the surface. In this respect many Centaurs, not only Chiron, go through the same process. First, and this can take the first half of one's life, the still dormant subconscious features of the Centaur, still trapped in a blind spot, cause not yet understood chaos and upheavals, emotionally and/or mentally. The true awakening often takes place after a crisis – not explainable by Saturn, Uranus, Neptune or Pluto, nor the progressed or solar return chart. Then somehow, often in unusual ways which can even involve the occult or drugs, Centaurian enlightenment is reached. And when ones character is developed strong enough to let go of past shells (impotent habits, infertile self control, obsessions, etc) a new life may start to happen.

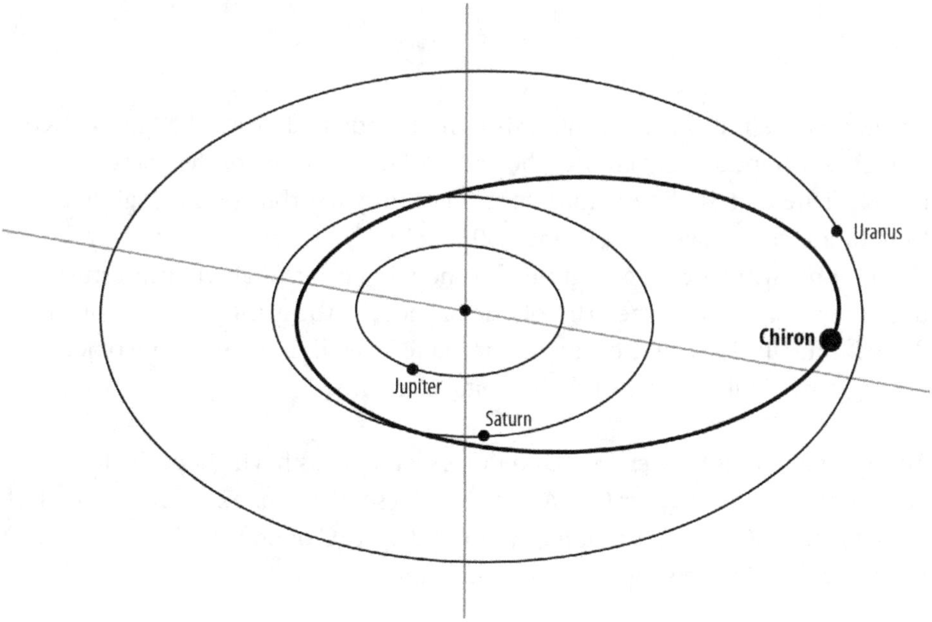

Orbit of Chiron

In general – because as I mentioned before, there are quite a few exceptions – Centaurs are the most complicated asteroid-class to deal with on the mental-psychological level. To make it worse (or more interesting), let's call in the help of our dear friends the astronomers:

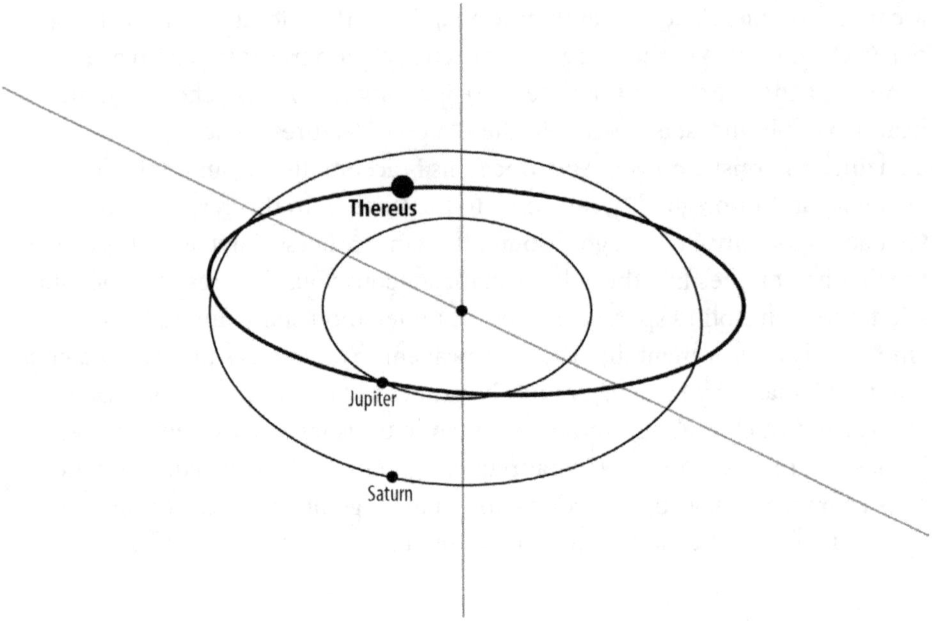

Orbit of Thereus

The generic definition of a Centaur is a small body that orbits the Sun between Jupiter and Neptune and crosses the orbits of one or more of the giant planets. Due to the inherent long-term instability of orbits in this region, even Centaurs such as 2000 GM137 and 2001 XZ255, which do not currently cross the orbit of any planet, are in gradually changing orbits that will be perturbed until they start to cross the orbit of one or more of the giant planets. However, different institutions have different criteria for classifying borderline objects, based on particular values of their orbital elements:

The **Minor Planet Center (MPC)** defines Centaurs as having a perihelion beyond the orbit of Jupiter (5.2 AU < q) and a semi-major axis less than that of Neptune (a < 30.1 AU). Though nowadays the MPC often lists Centaurs and Scattered Disc Objects together as a single group.

The **Jet Propulsion Laboratory (JPL)** similarly defines Centaurs as having a semi-major axis, between those of Jupiter and Neptune (5.5 AU ≤ a ≤ 30.1 AU).

In contrast, the **Deep Ecliptic Survey (DES)** defines Centaurs using a dynamical classification scheme. These classifications are based on the simulated change in behavior of the present orbit when extended over 10 million years. The DES defines Centaurs as *non-resonant* objects whose instantaneous (osculating) perihelia are less than the osculating semi-major axis of Neptune at any time during the simulation. This definition is intended to be synonymous with planet-crossing orbits and to suggest comparatively short lifetimes in the current orbit.

The collection **The Solar System Beyond Neptune (2008)** defines objects with a semi-major axis between those of Jupiter and Neptune and a Jupiter-relative Tisserand's parameter above 3.05 as Centaurs, classifying the objects with a Jupiter-relative Tisserand's parameter below this and, to exclude Kuiper-belt objects, an arbitrary perihelion cut-off half-way to Saturn ($q \le 7.35$ AU) as Jupiter-family Comets, and classifying those objects on unstable orbits with a semi-major axis larger than Neptune's as members of the Scattered Disc.

Other astronomers prefer to define Centaurs as objects that are *non-resonant* with a perihelion inside the orbit of Neptune that can be shown to likely cross the Hill sphere of a gas giant within the next 10 million years, so that Centaurs can be thought of as objects scattered inwards, interacting more strongly and scattering more quickly than typical Scattered-Disc Objects.

The **JPL Small-Body Database** lists 452 Centaurs. There are an additional 116 trans-Neptunian objects (objects with a semi-major axis further than Neptune's, i.e. 30.1 AU $\le$ a) with a perihelion closer than the orbit of Uranus ($q \le 19.2$ AU).

The **Gladman & Marsden (2008) criteria** would make some objects Jupiter-family Comets: Both Echeclus (q = 5.8 AU, TJ = 3.03) and Okyrhoe (q = 5.8 AU; TJ = 2.95) have traditionally been classified as Centaurs. Traditionally considered an asteroid, but classified as a Centaur by JPL, Hidalgo (q = 1.95 AU; TJ = 2.07) would also change category to a Jupiter-family Comet.

Other objects caught between these differences in classification methods include 944 Hidalgo, which was discovered in 1920 and is listed as a Centaur in the **JPL Small-Body Database**. (44594) 1999 OX3, which has a semi-major axis of 32 AU but crosses the orbits of both Uranus and Neptune is listed as an outer Centaur by the Deep Ecliptic Survey (DES). Among the inner Centaurs, (434620) 2005 VD, with a perihelion distance very near Jupiter, is listed as a Centaur by both **JPL** and **DES**.

The **Committee on Small Body Nomenclature of the International Astronomical Union** has not formally weighed in on any side of the debate. Instead, it has adopted the following naming convention for such objects: *Befitting their Centaur-like transitional orbits between TNOs and Comets, "objects on unstable, non-resonant, giant-planet-crossing orbits with semi-major axes greater than Neptune's" are to be named after other hybrid and shape-shifting mythical creatures.*

Thus far, only the binary objects Ceto-Phorcys and Typhon-Echidna have been named according to the new policy.

Lastly: possible dwarf planets raise further issues. Centaurs with measured diameters listed as possible dwarf planets according to Mike Brown's website include 10199 Chariklo, (523727) 2014 NW65, 2060 Chiron, and 54598 Bienor.

SCATTERED DISC OBJECTS

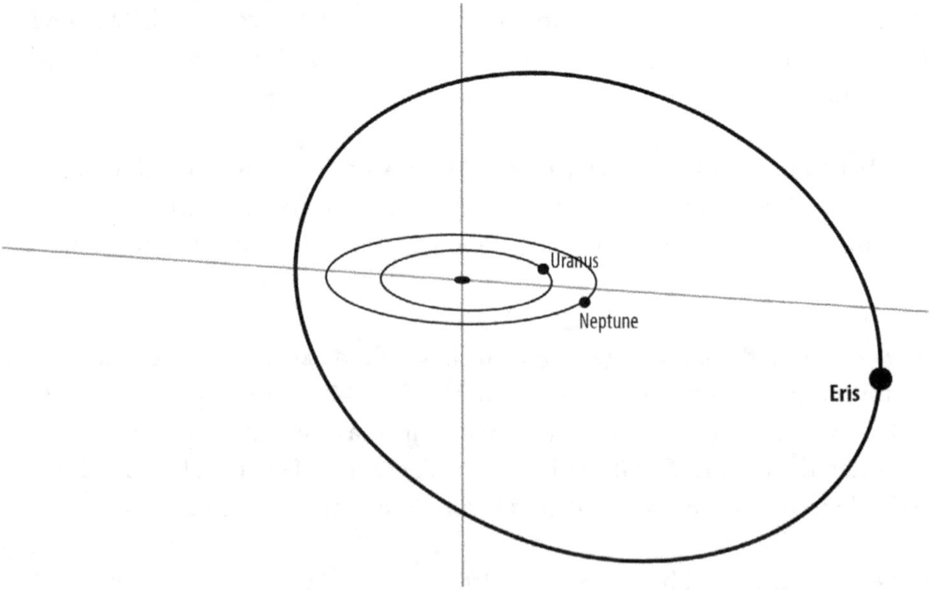

Orbit of Eris

The Minor Planet Center started to enlist Centaurs and SDOs as one specific class (Centaurs). However, from an astrologers point of view there is of course the duration-factor of the transit. The longer the transit, the deeper – on psychological (or practical) level – its influence. Sedna for example, when conjunct natal Sun has an effect very similar to a transit of (progressed) Moon through the 12th house, but much more intense in its isolating aspect, which can work pretty devastating when it comes to ones social-economic visibility. I don't need to explain to any astrologer that Sedna moves really, really slow.

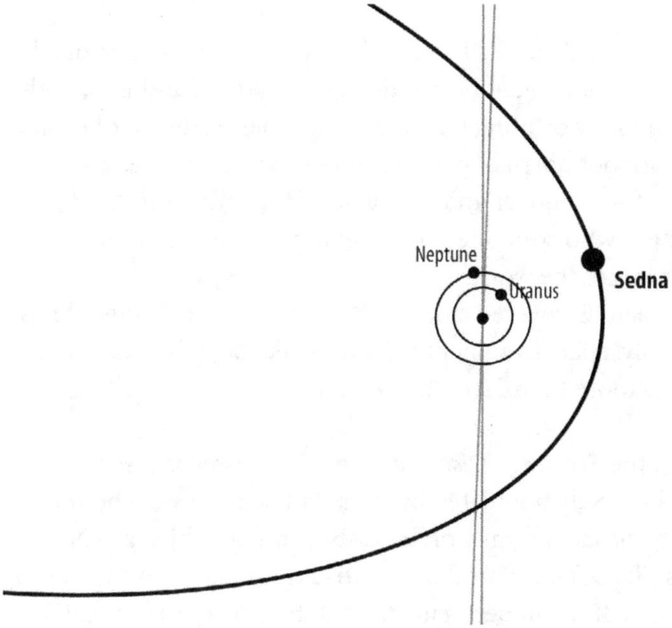

Orbit of Sedna

So one could say that, compared to Centaurs with their much shorter average orbital times (except Ceto-Phorcys) than those of SDOs, there is a substantial difference. Also, within our average human life span, many Centaurs – just like Chiron, when we reach the age of 51 – have their return:

- Biener at 66
- Chariklo at 62
- Echeclus at 35 – 70
- Elatus at 40 – 80
- ISON every 13 years
- Narcissus every 18 years
- Okyrhoe 24 – 48 – 64
- Pylenor at 68
- Rhiphonos at 35 – 70
- Thereus at 35 – 70
- 2000 BL41 at 30 – 60
- 2002 KY14 at 43 – 86

Elatus and 2002 KY14 join the Uranus opposition Uranus and Neptune square Neptune in the classic midlife crisis, while Thereus (*do not cage me!)*, Riphonos (*am I a man or a mouse?*) and Echeclus (*I am insecure but ambitious*) take care of the prelude.

So could we hypothesize that Centaurs more or less work out more personally than SDOs? Unfortunately that would be rather vague. Typhon and Eris, both SDOs, or at least extreme slow orbiting Centaurs, with their return far beyond the human life span, work out horribly personal and often as a two edged sword. Like in the case of warmonger and advocate of the Industrial Military Complex, Hillary Clinton, who combined the ongoing destruction of her inner life with that of many parts of the world.
About 700 SDOs have been discovered since 1995. But what is a Scattered Disc Object or SDO technically, apart from being Centaur-like objects with orbital periods that usually take more than 330 years to complete?

First of all, they orbit in the *Scattered Disc*, a distant circumstellar disc in the Solar System that is sparsely populated by icy small Solar System bodies, which are a subset of the broader family of Trans-Neptunian Objects (TNO's). Scattered Disc Objects (SDOs) have orbital eccentricities ranging as high as 0.8, inclinations as high as 40°, and perihelia greater than 30 astronomical units (4.5×109 km; 2.8×109 mi). These extreme orbits are believed to be the result of a gravitational "scattering" by Uranus and Neptune. SDOs continue to be subject to perturbation by these planets.

Although the closest Scattered Disc Objects approach the Sun at about 30–35 AU, their orbits can extend well beyond 100 AU. This makes Scattered Objects among the coldest and most distant Objects in our Solar System. The innermost portion of the Scattered Disc overlaps with a torus-shaped region of orbiting Objects, called the Kuiper-belt, but its external borders reach much further away from the Sun and far more above and below the ecliptic than the actual Kuiper-belt itself.

DETACHED OBJECTS OR EXTENDED SDOs

Detached Objects are a dynamical class of minor planets in the outer reaches of the Solar System and belong to the broader family of trans-Neptunian objects (TNO's). These objects have orbits whose points of closest approach to the Sun (perihelia) are sufficiently distant from the gravitational influence of Neptune, so that they are only moderately affected by Neptune and the other known planets: this makes them appear to be "detached" from the Solar System.

In this way, detached objects differ substantially from most other known TNO's, which form a loosely defined set of objects which have been pulled to varying degrees into their current orbit by gravitational encounters with the giant planets, predominantly Neptune. Detached Objects have larger perihelia than these other TNO populations, including the objects in orbital resonance with Neptune, such as Pluto, the classical Kuiper-belt objects in non-resonant orbits such as Makemake, and Scattered Disk Objects like Eris.

Detached Objects have also been referred to as Extended Scattered Disc Objects (E-SDO), Distant Detached Objects (DDO), or Scattered–Extended, as in the formal classification by the Deep Ecliptic Survey.

Because of its unstable nature, astronomers now consider the Scattered Disc to be the place of origin of most periodic Comets in the Solar System, with the Centaurs, a population of often icy bodies between Jupiter and Neptune, being the intermediate stage in an object's migration from the Disc to the inner Solar System. Eventually, perturbations from the giant planets send such objects towards the Sun, transforming them into periodic Comets. Many objects of the proposed Oort cloud are also thought to have originated in the Scattered Disc. Detached Objects are not sharply distinct from Scattered Disc Objects, and some, such as Sedna, have sometimes been considered to be included in this group.*

So, conform the latest theory, the Centaurs, SDOs – and Damocloids and (ex-) Comets – embody the most direct output of the evolutionary transformation of our Solar-System. Analogous to this process in the physical realm, from an astrological point of view *these objects cannot have another role to play but to question, irritate, attack, surprise, comprehend or shake up the modified reality.* This applies to the personal, (sub)cultural as well as mundane homeostasis, while in by far the most cases the end goal seems to be a new and higher – or different – state of order, similar to the process the Centaurs (and colleagues) are in; i.e. a process of getting stable orbits and non-oscilating perihelia. The reason why through the ages Comets were feared as bringers of bad luck or disasters can easily be placed in this context.

---

* *Source of astronomical specifics: Wikipedia: Scattered Disc Objects; Detached Object 09-24-2019.*

DAMOCLOIDS, RETROGRADE OBJECTS AND (EX-)COMETS

The best known Damocloids are Damocles, 127546 2002 XU93 and the retrograde-Centaur Dioretsa. Hidalgo looks astrologically like a small Damocles and is probably also a Damocloid. Damocloids are characterized by an extremely eccentric orbit, a reddish color and they behave like Comets without a tail (coma). About a hundred Damocloids have been discovered so far.

Retrograde-Objects are objects that are characterized by a retrograde orbit and an extreme inclination, which in some cases even makes their orbit almost perpendicular to the ecliptic. As with Centaurs and SDOs, there are mixed forms in their exact classification. For example, 65407 2002 RP120 is both a Damocloid, a retrograde asteroid and SDO. Astrologically Damocloids and Retrograde Objects in general have a closed-system-disturbing tendency and out-of-the-box thinking.

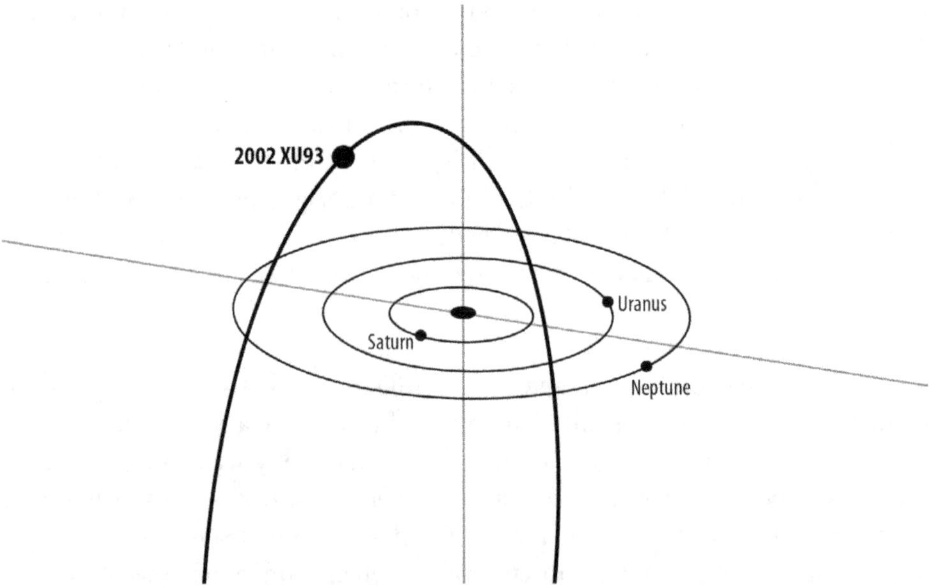

Orbit of 2002 XU93

(ex-)Comets or comet-like asteroids are characterized by asteroid-like behavior, but they differ from normal asteroids by still showing a weak coma (tail). Here too there are hybrid objects such as Chiron and Echeclus (classified as Centaurs in this book). 4015 Wilson-Harrington, 118401 LINEAR and 7968 Elst-Pizarro are classified as both asteroids and comets.

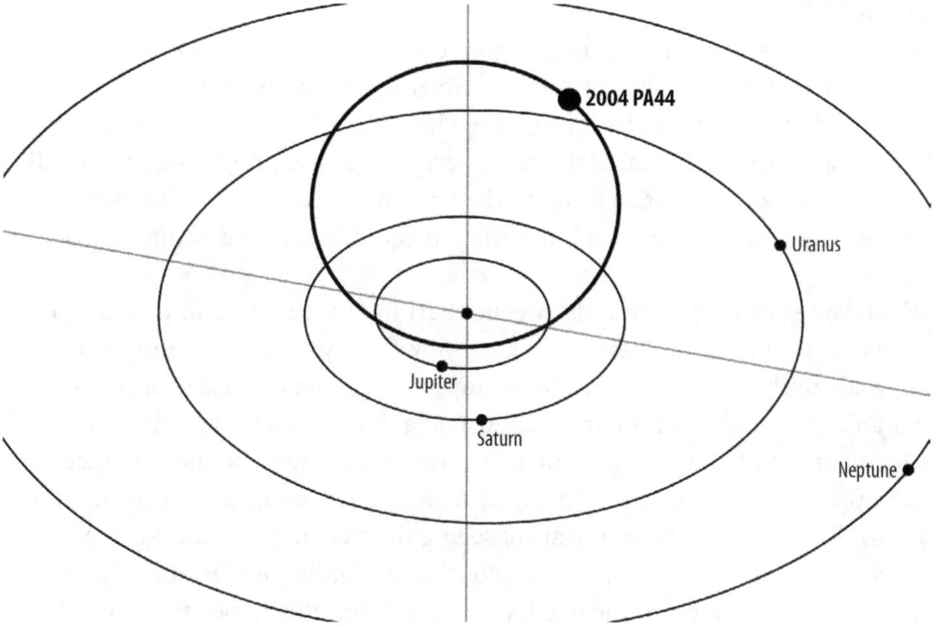

Orbit of 2004 PA44

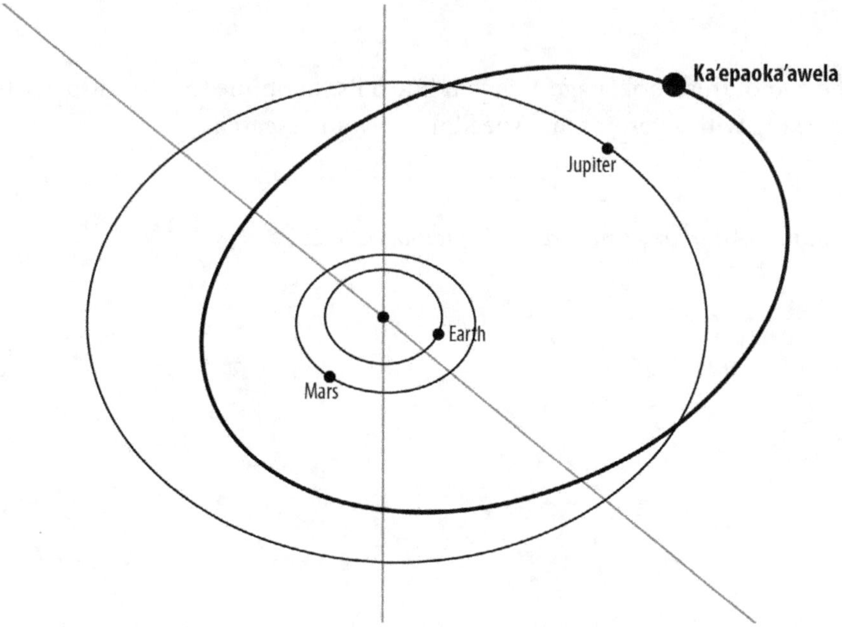

Orbit of Ka'epaoka'awela

SUMMARY

Although in general there is a significant difference between Centaurs, Damocloids, (ex-)Comets, Retrograde Objects, and the more Centaur-like SDOs and other classes of asteroids like Plutinos, Cubewanos, Haumeids, Trojans and Apollo, Hilda, Main-belt asteroids etc., each object has first of all qualities that are absolutely unique. The first volume of this asteroid-series begins with some of the most interesting, most dramatic and complex groups.

When you start using asteroids in your chart interpretations, do yourself (and your clients) a favor and start with just a few. Slowly extend the number of asteroids over a few years time. Most importantly (again!): use small orbs!! For an asteroid-aspect preferably apply half a degree before the minute exact encounter, up till half a degree after the exact encounter. Use the conjunction and opposition the most and study the trine and square later. The art of asteroid-astrology is the subtle art of seeing the tree in the forest, for there are many asteroids and they all have some sort of influence. Your choice of the asteroids you want to include has a Heisenberg-effect; meaning: just like the classic palette of the ten planets is a filter which determines the outcome of your reading, so is the classic palette expanded with asteroids. In any case: asteroids can greatly expand your astrological, psychological and philosophical horizons.

At the end of this book, page 157, you find a list of online tools, indispensable for working with asteroids and speeding up your research.

– Benjamin Adamah, Amsterdam September 25, 2019

FB 7

CENTAURS

55576 AMYCUS

Either a formidable or unscrupulous strive for power; verbal, psychological or energetic rape; lust and power play connections, BDSM; the personal power experience in relation to personal territorial boundaries.

Amycus moves within a weak 3:4 resonance with Uranus, and was automatically detected on April 8, 2002 by Near Earth Asteroid Tracking (NEAT). The diameter is 100.90 km. Amycus was named after a criminal and violent Centaur in Greek mythology, – who by rape and shattering someone's face – started the struggle between the Centaurs and Lapiths. Astrologically Amycus is a heavy weight, well capable of expressing the more brutal qualities of the mythological version. If dominant in the radix horoscope, Amycus may stimulate an insatiable urge for power, a tendency to manipulate, and it makes one verbally a fighter to the limit. There is no real respect for other people's boundaries, and even rape or assault is not excluded, although in almost all cases this is done psychologically and mentally. The game of power – even in its most cunning and ugly form and expression – is linked to lust and feelings of passion with a sexual undertone.

Amycus' discovery-horoscope shows a conjunction of Sun /Mercury / Eris / Siberia in the 19th degree Aries square Nessus (*rape*) in Capricorn and trine Pluto / Rhi phonos / Arawn in Sagittarius (*nervously aimed and focused at grabbing the power at the right moment*). Pallas is conjunct Eros sextile Sun / Mercury / Eris / Siberia and a conjunction of Machiavelli / Asbolus / Hermes in Capricorn (*cunning, dark urge for power and control*) trine 1998 XB (*sexual pleasure or extremism*). Venus is conjunct with the Saturnal Tukmit and aggressive Typhon (*infighting*) in Leo trine Varda (*impact, violent emotional outbursts*). The discovery-Amycus itself is in the 8th degree Libra conjunct Mors-Somnus / Rhadamantus (*overshadowing of justice*) / 2004 EW95 (*visionary*); trine 1999 OY3 (*relational intelligence*) and trine Rockefellia (*money and fame*); square Jupiter (*expansion*); sextile Ixion (*the intrinsic process*). Amycus has its discovery position in Libra opposition its discovery-Sun in Aries, indicating ambition whereby social connections are used to serve a selfish strive for power.

In the radix horoscope Amycus is obviously only a fraction of a whole and only when connected with objects or points that strongly catalyze Amycus' alter ego-energy in one's personality and social actuality, there is the possibly of a serious problem for the environment (and the person itself, because "Amycus unbound" is a kind of Devil's Pact in action, which will lead to total isolation). Amycus is richly represented in the BDSM-scene and among power politicians. Adolph Hitler had Amycus in Sagittarius conjunct Hylonome (*fusing extreme popularity with an extreme and aggressive manifestation of power*); trine Mercury in Aries; trine Taurinensis / Rockefellia (*military strategy backed by big money*) in Leo. I.G. Farben, the pharmaceutical company that built and managed Auschwitz, was a subsidiary of Rockefeller, and according to several historians was not bombed by the allied forces because of Rockefeller's influence.

Pro-NATO & Pro-EU dictatorship politician Angela Merkel has Amycus trine Venus (*to connect*) and trine Industria / 1993 SC (*always busy creating or nurturing trust bonds*). During a debate, such as in 2016 with Sahra Wagenknecht, Merkel showed her true anti-democratic face like never before, and her deliberate disregard of Wagenknechts' speech was so obscene that its video became a social media hit.

Godfather of sadomasochism, Leopold Sacher-Masoch had Amycus in 11 Taurus conjunct Ixion / Narcissus; trine Asbolus / Vertex in Virgo; square Zephyr (*decadent sexual pleasure*); opposition 2003 AZ84 (*extreme research*) in Scorpio and Socrates / Amor in Sagittarius (*philosophically defending an idiosyncratic vision of passion*) and inconjunct the cusp of the 8th house (*here: sexual extremes*) in Libra, precisely at the point (= epicenter) of a Yod.

Amycus denotes a point that provides information about a personal power source, or shows by which specific means or tactics one tries to gain and establish power. This does not necessarily have to be something negative, but may just occur as a "byproduct" of some personal achievement or ambition. Amycus conjunct an asteroid, which for example has to do with research, can lead to the acquisition of authority and prestige resulting from a discovery or scientific work. Opposites with Amycus indicate what other power (represented by a celestial body in the opposite house and sign) will act as "an undermining force or obstacle" on the way to personal power. In the radix chart, Amycus also displays ones personal power management in relation to personal territorial boundaries. Amycus-transits can temporarily manifest power struggles or issues. Amycus-afflictions in general are always about power and personal power and all the consequences and inconsistencies associated with power. Transneptunian-astrology.blogspot.com has associated Amycus with the anomaly that was latent in a system (Uranus exact conjunct Thule) while Mark Andrew Holmes links the Centaur to innocent victims of violence or getting caught up in violence. During the terrorist attack of March 22, 2016 in Brussels, Amycus was 6°57 Capricorn sextile Nemesis (*severe judgment, doom news*) at 6°57 Scorpio.

Amycus has an orbital period of 125 years and 270 days.

121725 APHIDAS

Provocation; emotionality linked to public performance; dissonant relations between government or public awareness and family or home situation.

Centaur discovered by C. W. Hergenrother, on December 13, 1999, conjunct – at the moment of discovery – with the star Procyon, with an estimated diameter of 76 km. The name Aphidas was given to Centaur 1999 XX143 in 2018. Ovid describes Aphidas in his *Metamorphoses* in the following fragment:

..Amid the noise, and tumult of the fray,
Snoring, and drunk with wine, Aphidas lay.
Ev'n then the bowl within his hand he kept,
And on a bear's rough hide securely slept.
Him Phorbas with his flying dart transfix'd;
Take thy next draught, with Stygian waters mix'd,
And sleep thy fill, th' insulting victor cry'd;
Surpriz'd with death unfelt, the centaur dy'd;
The ruddy vomit, as he breath'd his soul
*Repass'd his throat, and fill'd his empty bowl.. **

Aphidas, killed in his sleep as a punishment for his unacceptable misbehavior, reborn as an asteroid indeed emanates a provocative, rebellious energy basically in an emotional way and does so often in public. There is a generally dissonant relationship between public life and home or family situation. This is often the result of a government's distant mismanagement whose impact can hit the family severely. Nevertheless, if the person gifted with a dominant Aphidas refrains from the ad hoc ventilation of a crisis in the intimate sphere, triggered by whatever public cause, much is possible. Apart from the fact that

* *Ovid, Metamorphoses; Translated by Sir Samuel Garth, John Dryden, et al.*

Aphidas, in the first instance, tends towards provocative defense (or in case of an affliction, unconsciously creates reasons for this), there is also a strong urge to demand integrity and the possibility of growing and finding satisfaction, emotionally, affectionately and relational, or even becoming widely known to the general public. The fixed relationship with a life partner for a longer period of time, however, remains a difficult thing. But this can also come into good shape if the emotional impulsiveness is converted into well-founded, solid knowledge sharing, and, on that basis, stands for something. The energy of Aphidas regularly comes to the fore in the horoscopes of provocative pop artists, but it is best expressed in the horoscope of a writer, publicist or publisher. The relationship with the concept of family, though often capricious and unusual, can nevertheless be strong.

The orbital time is 76 years and 205 days.

8405 ASBOLUS

Soot, what is covered or gets stained or polluted by soot; negative creativity or creative negativity; something inhuman; horror, horrifying situations; the Satanic in both the perverted and metaphysical sense; a heightened consciousness; strongly rooted; root chakra awareness; increased awareness of privacy and personal boundaries and intuitive alertness of everything that may threaten the privacy and personal integrity; premonitions; an extreme sense of smell; the reptilian brain; the boundaries and bottom line of cognitive awareness; (with Phoinix) confrontations that require a radical change of thinking and attitude to improve one's status, break through a farce and reboot the flow of one's individuation process.

Asbolus was discovered on April 5, 1995 by James Scotti and Robert Jedicke and measures 66 kilometres in diameter (Jet Propulsion Laboratory observation, 2016). The Centaur shows a large impact crater and is named after the mythical Centaur Asbolos because of its dark surface. The Greek Ἄσβολος means *soot* (or carbon dust). Asbolos was the seer among the Centaurs in Greek mythology, whose correct warnings – not to fight the Lapiths – were ignored. In contrast, he later provoked a bloodbath in which Chiron and Pholus met their deaths at Heracles' hands. Asbolos was crucified by the demigod, who shot arrows through his limbs. Because of his second sight, he was described by Hesiodes with the nickname oiônistês (augurist – someone who predicts the future from the flight of birds).

Asbolus is a heavyweight; gloomy, pessimistic, with a lot of depth – and apt to becoming entangled in a vortex-like way of information processing – so that someone with a strong dominant Asbolus usually has a lot of trouble receiving advice or compliments from others. This is in essence a negative side effect of Nick Anthony Fiorenza's association of Asbolus with privacy awareness and a heightened intuition concerning threats to one's privacy. Within this context and connotation Asbolus easily goes over the top, exaggerates personal boundary control, and this alone gives an unnecessary state of isolation, so that even the positive can no longer enter ones system as a nourisher. Asbolus has a strong link to an extremely developed sense of smell, the darker niches of the occult, divination and, especially when afflicted, the Centaur seems to make one feel cursed in a way, by putting a damper on hope and life in general, thus replacing passion with feelings of heaviness or being overshadowed. Then Asbolus becomes a pair of eyes, glowing in the dark, searching for the light. When stuck in this worst case scenario, only radical self integrity leading to Vajrayana-consciousness (*identification with the atman or immortal inner flame*) can show the way out. The Centaur's discovery-horoscope is under a heavy influence of Orcus, Black Moon and asteroids with bridge functions to the paranormal (Sun conjunct Flammario, Summanus and Cerberus; opposite Nyx; sextile Moon / osc. Black Moon) with strong positions for Sundsvall, 2001 SQ78, 2001 UR163, 2005 UJ438, Lilith and Galahad. Venus is conjunct Sethos (*feeling cursed*) and Neptune is frustrated by a conjunction with the suicide asteroid Thisbe.

One could distinguish six different types or subtypes of Asbolian influence. The first type *detects* the inhumane, the perversion or violation of human rights and the ethical (Julian Assange, Jannis Varoufakis, Micha Kat, Edward Snowden, Sahra Wagenknecht, Karl Marx and others). In the second case, Asbolus is not strong and more a kind of dull black spot in the horoscope. In the third case, the seer aspects come out strongly (James van Praagh and Anton Pauwe). In the fourth case, Asbolus is a pit of horror, darkness, inhumanity (radix horoscope VS, Madeleine Albright, Joris Demmink, Adolph Hitler, Barack Obama, Zbigniew Brzezinski, G.W. Bush, Hillary Clinton, Joseph Stalin etc.). In the fifth case Asbolus is a dark artistic inspirator in a creative horoscope, making an impact on the public by mingling the aesthetic with some distorted, taboo breaking, or intense Plutonian atmosphere (Ilona Staller, H.R. Giger, Georges Bataille). The sixth Asbolus is a crossbreed of two or more samples of the above. For example, one could be a loving person, socially very aware of ethical values, but also a master in writing short horror stories.

When in league with evil, the outcome is never Asbolus' responsibility alone, but a joint venture with the totality of the chart, and its actual influence depends on the smallest nuances in the horoscope itself, in combination with influences that are not directly traceable for the astrologer, such as genes, educational details, media indoctrination, (sub)culture, food patterns etc..

Soot is what is left over after something is purged by fire or – psychologically – the Fire Element. It doesn't ascend (no enlightenment) but decends (is thus bound to concentric force; gravity). From a metaphysical point of view, it corresponds to, or represents – in a material form – the domain of Yin; ontologically and sociologically it relates to the root of individualism, technology and in the worst case: murder. Theologically (both from the cliché- and the Miltonian point of view) it relates to the figure of Satan. We also find the link between soot and evil in Monty Python's *Time Bandits* and the Hasidic story of the *Ba'al Shem Tov and the Coal Burner*, in which a lonely charcoal maker becomes so lonely that he becomes Evil itself – within an otherwise peculiar kind of vulnerability (intrinsic fear), which the Ba'al Shem exposes by not showing any fear himself, where nobody dared to approach the charcoal maker. Soot is a kind of coagulated, materialized absorption force of light including the light of life and everything that makes life light and, in a paradox, it consists mainly of carbon, the element all life on Earth is based upon.

Asbolus' "soot" is beyond the horizon where bodies with dominant concentric forces, like most Plutino's, are very strong and trigger transformations and deep changes in consciousness. Asbolus' "soot" lies in the area of total helplessness, the desolate, the bottom of the pit, waiting for external help from the camp of human kindness. As mentioned above, soot consists mainly of amorphous carbon particles. Carbon is the basis of biological life and its evolutionary outcome in human consciousness: *individualization* – thus subjectivizes the objective mind (the divine, trans-personal, and impersonal). Soot is mixed with carcinogenic PAHs, which associates it with aggressive growth, cancerous processes.

The geopolitician Zbigniew Brzezinski, an important player behind the scenes concerning American warfare and the abominations in connection with it, had Asbolus in the border dissolving sign of Pisces conjunct Typhon / Pest sextile 2001 FL194 / Logos (*charismatic, logical reasoning*). Georges Bataille, highly exaggerated nicknamed *the Philosopher of Evil*, had Asbolus conjunct Venus, and worked within a completely different vibe of this Centaur (which was appreciated by many of the people and artists he inspired) by being a taboo-breaker within a darkened Venusian zone of eroticism. Dani Filth, singer and lyricist of the very successful Gothic metal band *Cradle of Filth* has Asbolus in Leo, conjunct Amun (*ambition*) / 2004 EW95 (*penetrating vision*) / Sparks (*glitter, to shine*). He has a skeleton under a glass plate in his kitchen and a lot of humor when interviewed. Asbolus is richly represented in the scene of horror writers and filmmakers, Gothic and Black Metal artists and fans, and does little harm there. Philip Sedgwick finally associates Asbolus, in addition to the more commonly accepted associations, with omens, sensors and abstract logic.

Asbolus' orbital period is 76 years and 168 days.

54598 BIENOR

Great fame gained by hard "mission-like" work; group popularity resulting from achievements; perseverance; drive; excellent achievements or inventions, which have a shadow side or harmful side effects that are ignored, naively because of an immature mindset, or deliberately to avoid ethical and/or social confrontations.

Bienor is one of the larger Centaurs, measuring 187,5 km in diameter. The object was discovered by Deep Ecliptic Survey on August 27, 2000. Bienor means *strong man* in the Greek language. The Centaur has its discovery-Sun in 4°09 Virgo, conjunct Chariklo / Requiem / Skepticus / Verdun in opposition Bienor's discovery position at 3°30 Pisces and Manwë-Thorondor at 3°27 Pisces. Sun and Bienor are squared by Ixion / Asbolus/ Hygeia in Sagittarius, while Nessus is sextile to Bienor and trine Sun. Pholus is sextile to Sun and trines Bienor. The discovery-Moon is in 2°28 Leo conjunct Lucifer / Gorgo / Hephaistos / Alu; sextile Saturn in Gemini; opposite Neptune/1999 OY3; trine Ixion / Asbolus / Hygeia; trine 2005 UJ438 in Aries; sextile 2004 EW95 in Libra. Additionally Moon is sextile Rhadamantus.

Like Okyrhoe, Bienor has its discovery-Sun in the 4th house, and also like Okyrhoe its discovery horoscope denotes a strong ambitious drive and aspiration for a high status in public life. Yet these ambitions are often the cause of a dissonance between one's public and private life, the one not nurturing the other. Bienor exposes a higher sensitivity in emotional and relational matters than Okyrhoe. However, Mars square Juno in the discovery horoscope often poisons the fruits of this empathetic quality.

Bienor is first of all – like Hylonome, but in a different way– about huge popularity. Whenever Bienor connects a technical or craft performance

in one's horoscope to strong ambition, there is a great risk of ignoring the ethical issues and health damage accompanying the end result or beta versions. However, this is often simultaneously accompanied by the strange, almost surreal situation of an enthusiastic public, completely ignoring these unwelcome side effects and thus institutionalizing this dishonest, unfinished reality in such a way that it becomes almost impossible to discuss the topic once it has condensed itself – thus making the whole thing cancerous.
The discovery horoscope offers us an explanation for this weird situation: Backed by the combinations (Typhon / Aten; trine Industria / Varda / Thule), (Chariklo conjunct Sun) and (Gonggong trine Hylonome/2001 KF77) Bienor is easily perceived by the crowd as a visionary missionary, who by hard work and personal sacrifice of time, money and energy, created something groundbreaking and very important for our future. Bienor becomes a hybrid of an activist and a prophet with a mission, that is "cool" to follow because it fills up one of those typical postmodern identity vacuums. As a final finishing touch, Black Moon & Damocles conjunct Midheaven adds a "rebel image" to the illusion and saturates the whole situation with anxious excitement over future promises and new horizons.

Catalyzed by the Haumeid 2005 CB79 (Frankenstein-technology), nowhere have Bienor's intrinsic effects become more manifest than in the birth chart of Steve Jobs (Bienor conjunct MC in communication sign Gemini; trine Ixion in Libra; trine Atlantis in Aquarius). Millions adored the Big Man of Apple as Jesus Christ himself, while ignoring all the side effects of both Apple (*extreme exploitation*) and its products, which operate only on the basis of severely carcinogenic and generally harmful radiation.

Searching for an astrological answer to the question why certain people become known to a huge public and how, I examined 150 test-horoscopes of very famous or popular persons, both male and female. Bienor as well as Hylonome emerged as dominant factors in the results, with the difference that in cases where Bienor was dominant, the person in question worked hard for his or her position, while in cases where Hylonome was dominant usually no one has the faintest clue to where the popularity is based upon. In cases where Bienor aspects Hylonome, especially when in trine or in conjunction, we often notice an extreme popularity, as in the charts of Johan Cruijff and Steven Spielberg. To make a last reference to Bienor's discovery horoscope: Bienor is in sextile Vertex / Nessus (*inevitable breakthrough*) and the Vertex / Nessus conjunction is trine Sun in Virgo (*hard work, being industrious, eye for detail*). Yet I have clearly outlined the blind spot of this Centaur; when ambition and popularity start overruling the necessary reality checks, one ends up as a person who is constantly mixing a state of denial (and a survival-pack of institutionalized lies) with a pact with the (inner) Devil.

Bienor has an orbital period of 66 years and 329 days.

65849 CETO-PHORCYS

The conversion of what dwells in the collective conscious and unconscious into a mostly visually expressed Zeitgeist-report; one image saying more than a thousand words; perceiving the auto-destructive element in huge unconscious processes, developments behind the scenes and immense out of control movements within the social, ecological or (geo)political dimension; press photographers who show the excesses of socio-economic blind spots; the art of bringing the more dimensional context and connotation of a situation or process in synergy with the "eye catcher element", non personal gestalt-therapy.

Ceto (officially Ceto-Phorcys) was discovered on March 22, 2003 by Chadwick Trujillo and Michael E. Brown, and is an Extended Binary Centaur. It is binary because it consists of two separate bodies circling around a barry centre, and extended because it's perihelion lies beyond Neptune's orbit. The Centaur is named after Κητώ, Kêtő, *sea monster* in ancient Greek. Keto was the daughter of the Earth goddess Gaia and the sea god Pontus. Phorcys was Keto's brother and husband, with whom she had many children. Ceto measures 174 km in diameter and Phorcys is about 132 km. To give a small impression of her extreme orbit: Ceto crosses Uranus, where she comes closest to the Sun (perihelion), and from there she moves to a point about 4,5 times the distance Sun-Pluto (aphelion).

The astrological qualities of Ceto are both complex and subtle. Yet when applied by someone with a strong Ceto in the birth chart, who is as sensitive as intelligent, they can produce impressive creative achievements. Ceto is often strongly aspected in the horoscopes of press photographers who depict world shocking excesses of social-economic blind spots. A strong Ceto gives a person an extremely sensitive antenna for, what can be summarized as, *Zeitgeist-problems*. At first they are perceived unconsciously, but in the course of life this person realizes more concretely the difference between intrinsic reality (nature and authentic culture) and modified reality (trend indoctrinated mass culture) and their mutual interference. Ceto detects and or records huge unconscious *reality tectonics*, collective blind spots, the structures and strategies of political activities, kept secret from the public and cloaked by the mainstream media, auto-pilot constructions and processes which escape the attention, including their auto-destructive mechanisms. Ceto wants to point the attention to this, but someone with a strong Ceto usually has a long way to go before he or she is capable of finding the right medium, even if it is photography, film or text, which is also due to the complexity of penetrating the idea fixes of our default reality and the unconscious resistance of people to allow such radical changes of perspective. It's no wonder Ceto is strong among press photographers, documentary makers, research journalists and culture philosophers *depicting* ecological and socio-economic blind spots. I use the term *depicting*, because Ceto has this overlap with Neptune, being very visual in its expression. Translated into classic astrological terminology Mercury in Pisces in the 10th House would describe the nature of this Extended Binary Centaur pretty accurate – except this slow moving object can exert much more power. The highest Ceto-performance lies in convincingly depicting an alternative reality by exposing our consensus reality from an out of the box perspective. Movies like *Koyaanisqatsi* (Life out of Balance) and *HOME* are such typical Ceto productions, just like the World Press Photo of the *napalm girl*, taken during the Vietnam War. Ceto in action can perform the very difficult task of bringing the more dimensional context and connotation of a situation or process in synergy with the eye catching element.

Though not an explicit sexual asteroid, Ceto increases the sex drive and sexual fantasies, but at the same time makes it very difficult to communicate one's own needs and feelings, so that this aspect of Ceto often manifests as frequent masturbation and fantasies, which can be intense, or – especially when in a passive sign or passive house – may lead to porn addiction. The stream of inspiration is uninterrupted and continuous with a dominant Ceto and its visions and conceptions often seem to come from a totally different world. A negative side effect for persons with a strongly afflicted Ceto is feeling totally displaced, like being forced to live on a planet that isn't the one you came from. In extreme cases Ceto can stimulate suicidal thoughts, which are usually correlated to both perceiving the destructive element in the current reality mode, and fears for the future. Luckily, Ceto's discovery horoscope shows a prominent influence of Mars, in addition to the Neptune-like watery energies, which will usually prevent the actual act of suicide. The aversion to the crudeness and lack of vision among psychopaths, politicians, multinational CEO's, etc, who abuse the Earth and the social grid until nothing is left, is substantial, because this creates a continuous friction with Ceto's natural intuitive knowledge – of how our current default reality should be brought into synergy and symbiosis with the Earth and inner human progress. The precognition of unnecessary future disasters presents itself to Ceto in vivid pictures. Ceto can warn, especially through photography and film, and does that with a bang effect that reaches a large group (Uranus, ruler of Ceto's Discovery Sun, is conjunct Toro / Photographica / Gonggong).

Named after a mythical sea monster, several astrologers have associated Ceto with actual sea monsters, whales and large sea creatures in general. The discovery-ascendant trine Neptune / Scylla; sextile Charybdis and the Ceto conjunction with Leviathan in its discovery chart indeed give rise to this, as well as cryptozoology with regard to ocean animals. Deep-sea exploration, the remote areas of the cosmos, large unknown areas, and, to a lesser extent, the occult zones, also fall under Ceto. The occult is easily accessed with a strong Ceto by using psychotropic plants or mushrooms. (The discovery-Datura aspects Utopia, Ginevra, Flammario, Lilith and Yarillo – the latter denoting a link with chthonic fertility entities).

Despite being blessed and cursed with "the Eye of Odin", Ceto has a wonderful survival mechanism: a fairly strong sense of humor, which can transform the most repulsive information and actualities into satire, when the "sjen-qi" of one's system needs this protection or the social media environment is asking for it. Ceto can channel its true potential only through very talented people, and very proper circumstances. But when it happens the result is awesome because the public gets the feeling of being addressed by God Himself (or Goddess Herself, given the conjunction Haumea with the discovery-ascendant of Ceto). With a strong Ceto, there is a lifelong fascination for the sea, oceanic life, sea creatures, aquariums and everything underwater – even in the canals of Amsterdam – because the mystery of this hidden world lures and is magical. Cetos' psychosphere, as hinted above, also includes large sea creatures, especially deep sea creatures, whales, giant squids, kraken, monsters of the polar seas, such as the Greenland shark, etc.

The orbital period of Ceto is 1042 years and 79 days.

10199 CHARIKLO

Stretching horizons; creating space, rising beyond personal limitations; futurology, discovering new dimensions; science fiction; radiant personalities; broad mindedness with a strong focus on communication; trade and transport; affinity with education, teaching and the art world.

Chariklo was discovered in 6°04 Leo on February 15, 1997 by James V. Scotti. It is a very large Centaur, measuring 302 km in diameter, orbiting around the Sun between Saturn and Uranus. On March 26, 2014, the remarkable news was announced that Chariklo, like Saturn, had rings. The Centaur was named after the nymph Chariklo, daughter of Apollo and wife of Chiron. Chariklo is a predominantly positive and progressive force, which stretches horizons, creates space, opens up to new ideas, rises beyond the limits of personal constraints, broad-minded with a focus on the 'communication, trade, transport and travel-axis' Gemini-Sagittarius. Chariklo is further associated with visions of the future, futurology, the discovery of new dimensions and radiant personalities which easily create space and new perspectives where necessary. Chariklo prominent in the chart makes one physically, mentally and emotionally active and gives an affinity with education, teaching and the art world.

The Centaur easily harmonizes with groups and a fascinating study by Zane Stein showed that Chariklo has a strong link with science fiction, science fiction writers and science fiction actors, with a striking result for the crew of Star Trek. Chariklo has a strong connection with the creative and idealistic Leo-Aquarius-axis, in addition to the Gemini-Sagittarius-axis. Hereby, it is very important that the negative qualities of Leo (*egotism, egocentricism, feeling important for no reason*) are ignored to mobilize the totality of Chariklo's energy and direct it positively and in a creative way. Chariklo is ambitious (its discovery position is in the sign opposite the sign of its discovery-Sun), but not in the cold saturnal or plutonic manner, and usually lacks the obsession with status, excessive control and power.

Chariklo is more interested: *to boldly go where no one has gone before.* A strong Chariklo in the birth chart can periodically confront one with power issues or intense emotional situations, but these episodes usually end well. Chariklo greatly increases originality and ingenuity in a creative horoscope.

The orbital period is 62 years and 217 days.

2060 CHIRON

The personal blind spot; wound in the soul; (over)civilization; the identity crisis of people around the age of 51; shows gaps in one's individualization process and in what aspects it is malnourished; altruism; ingenuity applied for the benefit of others; usually a dislike of violence and love for civilization and cultivation; detached intelligence; wants to heal; when afflicted badly, a clinical, cold cruelty may manifest itself.

On October 18, 1977 Chiron was the first Centaur of this special class of asteroids that was discovered. The object was spotted by Charles Kowal. Chiron crosses the orbits of Saturn and Uranus and was estimated to be 166 km in diameter, but in 2011 the Herschel Space Observatory suggested a diameter of 218 km. Contrary to what was previously believed, Chiron does not contain ice, but interestingly has a weak coma, making Chiron a comet-like object, just like the Centaur Echeclus.

The mythical Cheiron (Ancient Greek: Χείρων) or Chiron (Latin) was the son of the Titan Kronos and the Oceanide Philyra. Cheiron was widely regarded as the "good centaur", by which he distinguished himself from the other members of his species. He appears as a teacher and mentor for several heroes, including Heracles, Jason, Aktaion, Achilles and even Apollo's son Askleipios, educating them as young men in music, archery, healing and art. Chiron was especially famous for his knowledge of medicine, which he passed on to Askleipios, but he was also an excellent sculptor. When Aktaion, one of his pupils, suddenly died and his dogs kept on barking and howling in grief, Cheiron comforted them by making a statue of their master. Cheiron was immortal, but when he was accidentally wounded by a poisonous arrow from Heracles, he passed his immortality on to Prometheus to release himself from his burning pains. Chirons' chart shows a civilized discovery-Sun in 24°52 Libra conjunct (a burned) Mercury / Pallas / Apophis / Pelion. The sign of Libra is a dominant influence in Chiron's nature, together with Venus. The 25th degree Libra is related to the transmutation of sexual energy but is also a Virgo-like degree, curious and investigating. The discovery-Chiron itself is conjunct Sedna (*taking distance from a situation or reality mode to see the whole picture*). Both North nodes are conjunct Pluto in Libra with the uncorrected Node just in Via Combusta and the corrected Node just not. This indicates a subcutaneous course away from the Mars-Saturn violence, very conscious of a world dominated by it, and therefore longing for the civilized alternative. With Orius on the MC, Chiron follows an (hippy-like) idealistic course. Within this context the rational and civilized Chiron is the civilizer who does everything in his power to bring things into harmony. The trine towards Huya in the discovery chart suggests that this striving extends to deep karmic patterns and past lives. This desire to bring things into harmony, to civilize and to get the best out of Libra is the basis of Chiron's association with holistic healing. (Supposedly dualistic forces are transformed into complementary forces operating in synergy). The burnt Mercury, Pallas and Pelion indicates Chirons' own blind spot. There is a lot of altruism, ingenuity at the service of others, but, while acting so, the Aries-element gets lost or eroded while the identity of someone with a dominant Chiron becomes more and more unbalanced and weighs heavily on service to others and situations. Many successful entrepreneurs enter an identity crisis around the age of 50/51 – coinciding with Chiron's return to the position in the birth chart. An acquaintance of me almost fills his entire therapy practice with this target group. All of them are "successful" in terms of social or financial *status*, while at the same time a now unbearable emptiness is felt inside. In most cases this is the result of never really paying attention to, and nourishing, their true needs, personal wishes and dreams, but sacrificing everything for their career. Suddenly the actual reality of their lives collides with this personal blind spot, alias wound in the soul, thus revealing itself. And at fifty, the best half of their life (energy and body) has been lived (in theory). Many marriages end in divorce around Chiron's return. Thus one could say that Chiron, returning to the position in the birth chart, begins his last project of holistic healing: that of healing one's own life.

In the thirty five years I practiced professional astrology, about 60% of my clients had the North nodes in Libra / 7th House and the South nodes in Aries / 1st House. Though I had a reputation for doing mainly the difficult (more interesting) cases, this suggest a very interesting astrological phenomenon from a statistic point of view, or at least it indicates that the balancing of this Libra Aries-axis is very difficult. In these horoscopes there is always a thorough correction of Aries-energy in process, but in the case of Chiron this process often goes over the top, forcing one in the first few years after the 50th birthday to make far-reaching adjustments, even if it means starting a new life with a new job and different partner. *In a paradox, Chiron then brings into consciousness what was brought out of balance by Chiron himself.* Chiron-energy going through this process can unfold a pattern quite opposite to the classic Chiron-pattern which is usually dominant in the first fifty years of our lives. The Apophis (the chronic fear we carry "under the skin") in Chiron's discovery-chart is entering into a pact with the Mars square Sun and Thereus / Machiavelli trine to Chiron's discovery-Sun. Pluto on the North nodes shows his other face and a formidable power is taking over. The most radical example of Chiron's alter ego (neglected by most writers on Chiron-astrology) we find in the chart of Adolf Hitler, who had Moon in 6° 32'54" Capricorn opposite Chiron at 6° 50' 1" Cancer, with Israel square at 5°43'18"Aries at their Midpoint and Moon conjunct 1996 TL66 at 7°02'25" Capricorn. * I sketch this caricature, in order to show the rebellious Chiron in the act of compensating *too much Libra* with *too much Aries*, in its most extreme form. Chiron's blind spot and hence the growth of a gap in our individualization process can be prevented by observing the (Mars-Venus / Aries-Libra / me-you) balance status in a chart *pragmatically*. The Aries / Mars factor should be brought into *synergy* right from the beginning with the many positive and altruistic qualities of this Centaur.

The orbital period of Chiron is 50 years and 131 days.

83982 CRANTOR

Unexpected terminations, positive or negative; sudden death – real or figuratively; the fragility of everything that is incarnated and alive; awareness of our transience and the emotion and vulnerability that lies therein – how we deal with the life-death contrast emotionally, psychologically, and on a mental and spiritual level; can act as a fatalistic force or trigger; a love for photography or to be photographed.

Crantor measures about 60 km in diameter, and the Centaur is currently orbiting in a 1:1 resonance with Uranus. Crantor was discovered automatically by Near Earth Asteroid Tracking (NEAT) on April 12, 2002 with its discovery position at 0°01 Scorpio and its discovery-Moon conjunct Eris / Pest / Sun in Aries trine cusp 8 / Vertex / Narcissus / Juno / Burney / Orcus in Leo trine Pluto in Sagittarius; opposition Lust / Huya, with Orcus in 8 opposition Eros. So in the nature of Crantor, we observe a strong connection between the Eros and Thanatos, underlining the myth that the Lapith Crantor is abruptly and mistakenly killed by the Centaur Demoleon *(Lion of the people)* during a wedding party.

Crantor in my opinion is mainly about the fragility of life and the fatality of death and how we deal with this contrast emotionally, psychologically, and on a mental and spiritual level. The notorious sudden end or death element often enforces contemplation within this context. Especially when studying minute exact transits to major players in the chart. Additional features of Crantor are: drug-triggered laughter kicks or death by overdosing the wrong drugs; aptitude for sexual astrology; increased risk of suicide linked to sentimental or narcissistic motives; interest in the magical and mysterious; premature death

---

* *Corrected chart data for Hitler: 20 April 1889, 17:29'40, Braunau, Austria. Chart correction based on Vertex/ Algol exact conjunction in 24°Ta40; 25 minutes before the exact Algol-occultation at 17:54'00.*

as a karmic setback, unexpected end, sudden death or closure, death by a spider bite or entanglement in a wrong network; sudden end or disappearance of partners or relationships or contracts, sudden death of the life partner, widows and widowers; drowning; alcohol poisoning; smoldering power conflicts and power-influence dissonances; death by explosion or a health problem, a hygiene error or illness that suddenly breaks out or breaks through; mourning cards, mourning correspondence, in memory of..., condolences and condolence registers; the magical command (directionism) in ritual magic, money magic, ban magic, necromancy; tax work. Finally, John Delaney links a love of photography or being photographed to Crantor, which I underline – after all, every moment is always dying acutely and photographs capture the moment and often very suddenly. Most astrologers underline the sudden end or sudden death as the main characteristic of Crantor. Additional associations are: interdependence (Phil Sedgwick), co-existence (Mark Andrew Holmes) and I have noticed these qualities manifesting in a dominant way during an exact square of Crantor to my radix Mars mixed with Delaney's local hero, when a dear friend of mine was fighting for his life in the hospital. Other associations are: the inhabitant who has lived somewhere for a long time, strong dedication, interest in cities, globetrotting, zones, zone laws, setting up zones, being a local phenomenon (John Delaney). In the radix horoscope, Crantor indicates in most cases through aspects and position, subjects, situations or areas that have been or will be linked to a sudden termination, closure or an abrupt shaking off of something. From a spiritual point of view, Crantor can make you deeply aware of the tenderness and vulnerability of physical life and the relationship between body, mind, soul, emotions, which as a whole are the person with whom we communicate, thus experiencing one's physical aspect as a given as mystical as the soul-, emotion-, or spirit contact. This Centaur makes us aware of our mutual transience and Crantor can intensify the emotion and vulnerability that lies therein like an exposed nerve. The Centaur especially reacts strongly to aspects with Mars.

The orbital period is 86 years and 44 days.

52975 CYLLARUS

Identity chaos; racism; protectionism; hostility towards politics that abolishes or blurs boundaries; financial strategy; a marriage or relationship with a partner that is very wealthy, or both wealthy and well known; experiencing one's own core as separate or detached from one's personality and personal motivation, resulting in a kind of chronically smoldering identity crisis; projecting inner uncertainties on others or groups.

Centaur of about 70 km in diameter, discovered by Nichole Danzl on October 12, 1998. With a dominant Cyllarus one can be very suspicious and may develop a certain cunningness, sometimes rooted in paranoia. Cyllarus makes one very aware of money and money-flows. This Centaur gives a talent for financial strategy, investments etc. and strives for as much economic independence as possible. A well placed Cyllarus in a chart, without too many "spoilers", also stimulates and promotes – however strange this may seem – a relationship with a partner who is either very wealthy, or wealthy and very well known. The home front is important and is well-kept and protected, and the connection with ones roots, birthplace or the country of birth is usually very strong when Cyllarus is dominant.

The Cyllarian personality has a built-in aversion against New World Order-politics which blurs or deletes the nation's borders and social-cultural frame. When afflicted, this quality may go over the top, and racist or aggressive and unreasonable nationalist tendencies float to the surface. Relationships with groups or group feeling tends towards the extreme, so in a bad chart racial scapegoating can be part of Cyllarus' output.

The root problem of this Centaur is the feeling that one's deepest inner core is separated from one's personality and personal motivation. This of course causes some kind of chronic identity crisis.
The discovery-Sun conjunct the fixed star Seginus in 18°33 Libra is inconjunct the Ascendant in 19°05 Taurus. And conjunct this Ascendant are: the discovery-Cyllarus / Altjira / and the Plutino's 1998 US43 (*identity / image dichotomy*) / 1998 WW24 (*autocracy*) / 1998 HK151 (*using NLP-techniques for power*). Chiron (*blind spot*) opposes the Ascendant and this cluster of minor planets. Alas, the inner insecurity and difficult to grasp identity lets itself easily translate into protectionist, discriminatory or racist politics, based – as usual – on distorted but often popular arguments.

However, the hidden subcutaneous course of Cyllarus – in contrast to the above – heads towards true inner stability and order, and proceeds through a Saturnal stabilizing energy. Yet, simultaneously there is a tendency for this energy to degenerate into disturbing or aggressive behavior or sexual abnormalities (North node conjunct Pheckda in 0°20 Virgin sextile Tukmit; trine Saturn). Cyllarus can waste a lot of energy to imaginary threats. On the other hand the threats can be real. Bruce Lee had to deal with racism and protectionist behavior all his life, being "a quarter" German and "three-quarters" Chinese – while he himself did a lot to transcend racial conflicts through his sport and bring this message to the people around him. He had Cyllarus in 19 Libra opposition Black Moon in Aries.

The orbital period is 133 years, 117 days and 12 hours.

60558 ECHECLUS

Uncertainty; a broken, disintegrating or crumbling basis; power issues; an urge to achieve something that gives prestige; holding on to the wrong things; stalkers; sticky things, glue, everything that is glutinous; lubricants; homosexual or bisexual encounters; mental late-bloomers; creating conflict or harmony / synergy between the big picture and the details; gestalt therapy; a craving for intoxication; periods of optimism, which have a positive effect on everything; wrestling with self-integrity and social integrity; "contagious" anxieties of the life partner that hinder one's strive for inner perfection and individuation; Vajrayana; chaos magic; launching a new order after a disastrous period of chaos.

Echeclus is a complex comet-like Centaur, which was discovered on March 3, 2000 by Spacewatch. Like Chiron, Echeclus has a weak coma, which is characteristic of comets. Its comet indication is 174P / Echeclus. It measures 59 km in diameter. The mythological Centaur Echeclus was killed by Ampyx in the battle with the Lapiths at the wedding of Pirithous, by being rammed in the face with a spear that had lost its point. If the spear hadn't lost its point, death would have occurred quickly and definitively. Instead, Echeclus' death came by multiple blows. The name Echeclus is related to *glutinous*.

The astrological meaning strongly suggests the following options: a constant state of uncertainty; a broken or crumbling base; power issues; an urge to achieve something that gives prestige; holding on to the wrong things, situations or ideas; stalkers; sticky things, glue, everything that is glutinous; lubricants; homosexual or bisexual encounters; mental late-bloomers; creating conflict or harmony / synergy between the big picture and the details; gestalt therapy; a craving for intoxication; periods of optimism, which have a positive effect on everything; wrestling with self-integrity and social integrity; "contagious" anxieties of the life partner that hinder one's strive for inner perfection and individuation; Vajrayana; chaos magic; launching a new order after a disastrous period of chaos; a certain craving for alcohol and drugs; conflicts between the spiritual and state religion(s); detecting collusion and government lies in official statements; an increased risk of becoming suicidal. When afflicted, a strong Echeclus may turn a person in a stalker or the ex-partner may become a stalker, or the person or one's partner may have to deal with persecution. This is often flanked by obsessions, difficulty concentrating or a neurotic tendency to always focus on the negative. Echeclus is also associated with the necessity to cultivate positive Leo-faculties; the Vajrayana or the Nirguna-experience as a last resort. It also has a link with applying magic after a disastrous personal crisis; aloofness from social events; an intelligent philosophical overview of technical developments regarding the Zeitgeist; launching a new order in general. Echeclus is usually unfavorable for a happy domestic life or happiness in general, especially when in the 4th house. Germany or relations with Germans either attract bad luck and are doomed to fail or in contrast, they lead to spiritual enlightenment, initiation or deep insight (Germania conjunct the cusp 12 in the discovery chart).

The influence of Damocles in Aquarius square Saturn in Taurus in the discovery chart, along with the Sun-Pluto square is substantial, with Sun sextile the damaged Saturn. This aspect-cluster together with Mercury / Salacia in Pisces opposition Logos in Virgo is urging the quest for *the inner Sun*, the atman, the Vajrayana state, i.e. peace, inner stability and forces one to set out one's own (positive) course in life, based on integrity (North nodes in Leo conjunct 2003 CO1). The chains of false certainties, mind frames, ties and illusions have to be broken just like the transformed caterpillar sheds its cocoon to become a butterfly. The discovery-Sun is conjunct Leviathan (*the big lie, official falsehood*), conjunct Virtus (*virtue*) and Minerva (*wisdom, intelligent insight*).

Someone with a very dominant influence of Echeclus in the birth chart will discover, with the necessary luck, somewhere in his or her life, that an always felt urge to move forward and to reach a top level position in something (discovery-Echeclus in opposite sign of discovery-Sun) is, at the deepest and purest level a longing for the status of Vajrayana, total self-integrity, the rejection of all lies and illusions. As the latter is the only real – *independent* – top level position one can reach in life. With a dominant Echeclus, once having reached this state, a formidable self-determined force is released (Bennu opposition Skuld = *resetting your life by realizing that your proactive attitude determines your future*). Skuld is conjunct BAM, indicating that this transformation in consciousness comes with a deep impact and rather suddenly. Therefore, the mature Echeclus has a strong link with chaos magic, thought form magic and magic in general, especially with the aspect of directionism (giving a magical command). In forensic astrology Echeclus can also indicate a family of jumping spiders or a moth. The jumping spider is a very suitable animal to represent the chaos magical process in general. It is a symbol for the domain of the Yin-vortex in a torus model (described in my 2012 Dutch publication *Vamachara*) and the explosion (expansion from the yang domain), following this implosion. The latter (total identification with the domain of Yang, the active starting point in every authentic creative process) is the exact point the magician occupies in any magical operation.

The orbital period of Echeclus is 34 years and 329 days.

31824 ELATUS

Chameleons; negative fusing; smooth talkers; brokers; ego or identity development; a dissonance between passion (Eros) and sexual need and expression, which can derail or become perverse; no faith in politics; impressive; a talent for speaking with impact in a manner which however may leave the listener(s) in a state of confusion or chaos; marital problems; the overcoming of emotional dependency and relational parasitism, or making oneself guilty of it; imaginary acceptance-rejection issues and playing the enthusiastic smooth operator as the expression of one's survival mechanism.

Elatus was automatically discovered on October 29, 1999 by the Catalina Sky Survey and measures approximately 57 km across. Elatus shows a commitment to achieve something, reach a certain social status or to distinguish oneself. Elatus can bestow a natural magnetism on someone, making the person quite easily charismatic, popular or known to large groups. This works more or less automatically, while no one really understands the "how"or the "why" or the lack of qualifications of the "Elatus-dominant in the chart-type". Typically for Elatus, the top position is therefore often a false position. Elatus makes one very sensitive with a tendency to emotional dependency and even to be exploited on the basis of trust. There is a penchant for booze and a talent for trouble that started with uncontrolled drinking, as well as attracting a drug addicted partner of the borderline type. Elatus creates a dissonance between passion (Eros) and sexual needs and expression, which can derail into the extreme and bizarre. Mark Andrew Holmes mentions Elatus in the case of Kevin Eugene McAfee, who was caught having sex with a mare. In the discovery chart of Elatus, Nessus (*rape, assault*) is conjunct cusp 6 (*domestic animals*). The discovery-Moon is on the midpoint Lovejoy | Schadow (Moon making a trine with both asteroids); opposition 2002 PN34 (*parasitism*); sextile 1988 XB (*extreme sex*) and conjunct 2001 XA255 (*judicial persecutions*). George Bataille had Elatus conjunct 1988 XB / Saturn / Uranus in Scorpio.

Additional features of a strong Elatus are: no faith in politics; impressive; a talent to speak with impact in a manner which however may leave the listener(s) in a state of confusion or chaos; marital problems; the overcoming of emotional dependency and relational parasitism, or making oneself guilty of it; a strive for power and control over situations, rooted in a strong urge to leave a chaotic condition behind or to change it. This latter feature shows the inherent core-drive of the so easily derailing Elatus. The North nodes are conjunct Tukmit in Leo in the 1st house trine Pluto / Ginevra / Vertex in Sagittarius. There is a desire for management and control, which is remarkably enough sometimes coupled to female ghosts or spirits (Ginevra) or occult events (Flammario also trines the Nodes). Arachne (*networks*) and Taurinensis (*military strategy*) are on the cusp of the 4th house, with house-ruler Venus on cusp 3 and 1998 BU48 (*the monetary flow*) sextile cusp 4. The communication / information / transport-axis 3rd house – 9th house is squared by Hidalgo (*taking unpredictable risks, walking on thin ice*). This can result in a smooth-speaking real estate agent whose sales are always rattling, or an insane home situation in which people strategically interact along the lines of a bizarre emotional network or an extremely exaggerated etiquette (Cusp 4 in Libra), in which they always walk on eggs in order to maintain a false sense of peace.

The primary or most spontaneous action emanating from Elatus is that of the usually *enthusiastic smooth operator*, who operates in a way that is usually perceived as pleasurable and enjoyable, but who eventually makes a mess of everything. Projects or deals are not well thought out, not well prepared or there are skeletons hiding in the closet, held in place with duct tape. The inner core process of someone with a problematic Elatus can best be summarized by "Get real!" When the emotional life depends entirely on reacting on others or the outside world and dependency on others, without any legitimacy to the inner core, (Sun, atman) there is an awkward split, too big a gap, between the persona and the "I". Elatus dominant often gives a persona that is much stronger than the inner self or "I", producing an inherent dissonance in the persons character. Perhaps for this reason the North nodes in Elatus' discovery chart are in the first house in Leo. The mature Elatus is not undetermined (the negative Libra), does not sell daydreams (the negative Aquarius) and is extra alert regarding situations where others manifest these vices. The immature Elatus is like a chameleon who adapts to everyone and everything and hides certain secret, private delights. In the natal chart Elatus denotes where and how imaginary acceptance-rejection issues play. House, sign and aspects specify the details of this dilemma. The Centaur also indicates certain desires or habits kept private.

Finally Elatus gives information about the *why* or in *what* circumstances, or correlated to *which* challenges, people feel themselves not yet ready or worthy to express and manifest certain talents, resulting in keeping them latent. Elatus reacts with its Moon-like absorption capacity strongly on the features of the zodiac-degree it is positioned in, whereby one tends to distance oneself from the psycho-spherical information of the preceding zodiac degree. The information of the degree in which Elatus is located is of great importance to a person's actual life and affinities. The degree that follows denotes a next level, something to work towards. That is to say, one examines how one can make the useful qualities of this degree one's own.

The orbital period of Elatus is 40 years and 157 days.

10370 HYLONOME

Incomprehensible popularity or immense celebrity; calculating; charisma; glamour; darling of the mass media; fashion or tabloid-star; star allures; beauty pageants; childhood idols; MTV-stars; artists or children of famous or wealthy parents hyped by marketers; commercial idol creation, mass hype in general; speaking the media trainers language; media trainers, spin doctors.

Hylonome was discovered on February 27, 1995 by David C. Jewitt and Jane Luu and its discovery position was 4°43 Libra in close conjunction with the "honor and respect-star" Eta Virginis at 4°46 Libra conjunct cusp 11. Hylonome measures 74 km in diameter, and was named after the female Centaur Hylonome which mourned her beloved husband Cyllarus. Chart-ruler Venus is conjunct Neptune / Pelion / cusp 3 / Ate / Amun / Ginevra / Actor / Uranus and the star Terrebellum (*favorable for finance, calculating*). Jupiter is in Sagittarius in 1 as ruler 2 trine Lovejoy in Leo and sextiles Narcissus and Mercury conjunct Moon in 3 in Aquarius. The Scorpio-ascendant makes a conjunction with Thereus / Nessus / Ixion / Pluto / Quaoar and is sextile and trine with the communication-axis 3rd house – 9th house. Gonggong (*group consciousness*) is in sextile aspect with cusp 2 and trine cusp 8. Saturn is conjunct Achernar, socially one of the most fortunate stars in the firmament.

The features of Hylonome, especially when conjunct Sun, Midheaven, ruling planet, Moon or ascendant, are: popularity, huge popularity and fame, being (world)famous or popular without having done anything substantial to gain this position or being popular while no one can understand or explain why; darling of the media, fashion and gossip magazines; a star-like allure, beauty pageants, youth idols, MTV stars, by marketers hyped artists or children of famous or wealthy parents, commercial idol creation, mass hype in general, Paris Hilton-like phenomena and hypes, earning a lot of money at an early age, a huge need for attention, to be too big for ones boots, speaking in media trainer coordinated language, playing the role of popular person very well and knowing how to shine; media trainers, spin doctors, things that go smoothly, youth careers.

I referred to Hylonome in the paragraph on Bienor because in a statistical research I did, involving 150 charts of very famous people and celebrities pointed either to a strong Hylonome or Bienor or both. In the latter case they were extremely famous. In case of Bienor this status was usually the result of hard work and perseverance. With Hylonome dominant in the chart, the work of an MTV or tabloid-manager who pushed and orchestrated everything, or some other kind of spinning process, or just stupid luck, like getting discovered on YouTube with boring vines, was usually the secret of success and the huge popularity. A popularity that remains a complete mystery for normal intelligent people, who cannot understand why carrying a chihuahua in your purse and waving at people, should be something everyone talks about.

One could psychologize Hylonome, but the question is whether this is very useful. If Hylonome links strongly with certain other bodies that are more strongly connected to a certain kind of talent, action, work, position, etc., Hylonome can easily give a quick lift to popularity and money, like some sort of intrinsic push-force. This is really astonishing, when you investigate this Centaur in celebrity birth charts. To make a long story short: if Hylonome had not been named yet, I would have been the first to suggest the name Paris Hilton for this Centaur. However, I do not want to withhold a number of additional associations, stuck to Hylonome by other astrologers: eternal youth, longing for a lost paradise, lost innocence, political and religious messianisism (Juan Antonio Revilla); longing for the impossible, reaching for the stars and landing on the Moon, frequency changes (Laurence Lucas); thrill seeking (Jonathan Dunn); an exceptional need for acceptance, lack of self-esteem, pathos, devotion, the ability to evoke sympathy or empathy, an increase of the emotional element in a situation, the perception of attractiveness, misfortune or helplessness, the desire to protect, defend or help others, fastidiousness, naiveté, softheartedness, catholic tastes and interests, a bent toward "naturalness" and environmentalism, an interest in fashion and adornment, criticism of others in order to appear good or strong, ability to help others through self-criticism, self-deprecation, dealing with grief and loss, and feminism in sexual partnership, without rejection or antipathy of males (Mark Andrew Holmes).

I guess there are charts that go easily with the Hylonome-flow and charts that challenge the Hylonomian fame with a series of reality-checks. The latter charts could become quite challenging as being a Centaur, Hylonome will have its own healing process. It will be clear what this process is all about, and yes, it may very well involve mourning, most probably about a phase in one's own life that had to "die" to become more real and less defined by others, or cameras or magazines etc.

The orbital period is 126 years and 221 days.

365756 ISON

The creative revolt, the artistic revolutionary; being popular because of idiosyncratic opinions, judgments or remarks; the prevailing consensus in which one moves is experienced as a constant field of tension, in which the pressure is always shifting; rich in inspiration; using playful, sympathetic, original forms of artistry and creativity to criticize social or political issues; the ability to radically and suddenly alter one's understanding of life or the course of one's life.

ISON was discovered on November 4, 2010 by Leonid Vladimirovich Élénine and was named after the *International Scientific Optical Network* (ISON). At the moment of discovery ISON was conjunct the Moon-Venus-like star Epsilon Tauri (*artistry*), 2001 SQ73 (*pressure changes, enter into discussion*) / 2003 VS2 (*fuck the system*). The discovery-Sun is in 12 Scorpio conjunct Okyrhoe (*acceleration*) and Icarus (*inspiratory flow*); opposite Industria; trine Zephyr / Summanus (*sensual-gothic decadence*). Mercury in Scorpio trines Jupiter in Pisces and Varuna in Cancer. Mars is conjunct Eros; Venus is conjunct Bacchus and sextile Pluto, whilst Pluto trines Orcus / Skuld. Pallas / Varda / Narcissus / 2001 KF77 are in opposition with1998 US43.

The following characteristics refer to the interpretation of a dominant ISON: artistic, multi-creative; out of the box, off the grid; society, system or prevailing consensus is experienced as a constant field of tension, in which the pressure is always fluctuating; the inspiration is very rich, possibly anachronistically oriented with a preference for Gothic, black romanticism, decadence, erotic, burlesque; psychotropic plants or mushrooms increase creative and spiritual insights or are problematic (Datura trine Neptune / Chiron); aid for drug addicts; raising an issue when one detects a dissonance between the image or persona of people or public figures, political parties etc. and their identity (Sigmund Freud had a strong ISON); using playful, sympathetic, original forms of artistry and creativity to criticize social or political issues; suddenly being able to radically deviate from insight or one's course of life; libido, erotic affinity, heightened sexual drive; aptitude for a very rich, visual, imaginative and colorful use of language and the translation of psychic and astral impressions into the right choice of words and wording; interest in the paranormal.

The orbital period is 13 years and 244 days.

37117 NARCISSUS

Selfishness or self-centeredness as a blind spot and obstacle to creativity; desire for status and grandeur, "aristocratic display"; a predominantly conservative vision, while remaining open to spiritualism; tends to assume a leadership role, in which one, however, continuously has to deal with unexpected situations every time one thinks to be on a solid course; a conflict between intuition and ratio; selfies, narcissism.

Narcissus was discovered on November 1, 2000, by William Kwong Yu Yeung and measures about 11.2 km in diameter. The name is derived from the Ancient Greek Narke (Νάρκη) and Narkissos (Νάρκισσος), meaning: *sleeping* or *numbness*. In Greek mythology, Narcissus was a hunter from Thespiae in Boeotia, who was renowned for his beauty. This spoiled him in such a way, that he despised those who loved him, proud as he was of his own good looks. Nemesis saw this and lured Narcissus to a pond, where he saw his own reflection in the water and fell in love with it, not realizing that it was only a picture. Narcissus died, not in a position to escape from the fixation on himself. The term narcissism was derived from this myth. With the asteroid Nemesis conjunct the North node (*karmic destiny*) in the "sign of ponds", Cancer, the Narcissus discovery chart is pretty consistent with this myth. The features of a dominantly aspected Narcissus are: selfishness or self-fixation as a blind spot and obstacle to creativity; desire for status and grandeur, "aristocratic display;" a predominantly conservative vision, while remaining open to spiritism; tends to assume a leadership role, in which one, however, continuously has to deal with unexpected situations, every time one hopes to sail a solid course. In forensic astrology Narcissus can denote: selfies, narcissism or daffodil (*narcis* in Dutch).

When active and busy, the energy is also very difficult to control, thanks to a mess of strange, sometimes dark hunches or feelings, partly due to an overcritical attitude that turns details inaccurately into main causes or concerns, partly because of a conflict between intuition and sober reason, between which one finds oneself in a dilemma. Trying to solve this conflict usually drains a lot of energy. The problem of keeping a steady course in life until an aspired respectable position in society is realized, is mostly due to a Sun-Damocles square in the discovery chart and an Eros-Black Moon conjunction in Capricorn which trines a Mars in Virgo and Saturn / Chaos in Taurus. Eros, the passion is purged, and so is the (status-)sign of Capricorn. In addition, Venus conjunct Chiron / Uranus (*altruism, homosexuality*) sextile Arawn (*einzelgängers, emotionally overreacting*), stimulates a rather unusual or difficult love life. Based on the position of Photographica, Narcissus at a lower octave has a relation with taking selfies. The Narcissism-theme in case of the Centaur Narcissus is mainly expressing itself in situations or an attitude where decorum, display or status are blocking the development of one's inner life. Thus distorting the full development and expression of one's individuation process. One can become so blinded by this, that one even loses contact with what is really one's true passion in life. A blind spot (Chiron) can easily appear when entering into a new relationship, due to being extremely self-centered and neglecting or refusing to broaden one's social and emotional scope (Arawn). Finally Narcissus has a link with the concept of rebirth or re-birthing, and there is a playboy-like, decadent or decadent-erotic element. When the energies of Capricorn and Aquarius have been purged, Narcissus may speed up the process towards fame or public recognition, especially if Narcissus succeeds in cultivating warmth toward others. Status must be obtained honestly. After all it is either a gift from the public as a token of appreciation, or nothing but empty self-delusion.

The orbital period is 18 years and 7 days.

7066 NESSUS

Border issues and border conflicts; beauty & beast polarity; forcing the access to something; burglary, hacking, phishing; penetrating and/or abusive; wounds or communicative deformations in the social aspect of sexual approach and expression; rape, sexual assault; to cause chaos or a rupture in closed systems and disintegrate them; a lasting poisoning of something; being extra aware of the power of life energy, the healthy or therapeutic use of sexual energy; blood, blood diseases or blood rituals; superhuman strength; black magic, blood magic; juju magic.

Nessus is a lump of ice of about 60 km in diameter, discovered on April 26, 1993 by David L. Rabinowitz in 5° Scorpio. This Centaur involves a lot of what you might summarize as third chakra issues, and it usually has a disorderly sexual imposition. Keywords such as *sexual assault*, *abuse* and *rape* cover many of Nessus' charge on the negative side. I repeatedly noticed a damaged Nessus in the fourth house in the charts of women who were sexually abused in childhood.

The core issue of a dominant Nessus is the difficulty in expressing oneself in relation to the other, because somehow one has the feeling or illusion that the other person wants to invade the personal privacy of one's own being. Paradoxically this is unconsciously or consciously reacted to by crossing the personal boundaries of the other. The deformation in Nessus' communication is therefore connected to the concept of *forcibly accessing* someone's psychic and energetic or even physical being.

Then there is a schizoid twist in Nessus due to the conjunction of Mercury with the Plutino 2002 VR128 trine Chiron in the discovery-chart, which balances Nessus' raw, brutal and sinister expression with a very human and spiritual mind and sensitivity. Therefore, due to this contrast – and only second to the notorious Pylenor – Nessus is one of the most dramatic and dark romantic of all Centaurs. Several researchers have associated Nessus with the Beauty & The Beast theme. Others have noticed links with schizophrenia, psychoses, occultism, prolonged skin diseases. The energy of the 8th house is very strong in Nessus and to make things worse Nessus often has an obsessive tendency to want to put things right, often coupled with the urge to do this openly and very demonstratively. This is a consequence of the conjunction Rhadamantus / Hylonome on cusp 9 in the discovery horoscope. Underneath, and when not self sabotaged by emotional aberrations, Nessus wants to work his way up and is very ambitious, as indicated by Nessus' position almost exactly opposite Sun in the discovery-chart.

Nessus is one of the few newcomers in astrology that has been observed and studied for quite a while. Considering its complex and rather extreme nature, it is no wonder we see a large diversity in the collection of attributed characteristics; lessons in setting boundaries, seeing (one's own) limits, accepting limits; identification of hidden abuse patterns; complex cause and effect relationships, breakpoints in karmic cycles; revealing the truth, resolving a situation; taking responsibility for a confrontation, the perpetrator caught; desire; possessiveness, jealousy, being vindictive, manipulative or resorting to black magic for sexual or financial needs. Finally, several researchers associate Nessus with blood, diseases passed on by blood, or blood rituals, and superhuman strength or powers. Philip Sedgwick characterized Nessus as "The ultimate Centaur bad boy", bearing the wounds of "greed, decadence, intimacy and sexuality". As positive Nessus properties he mentions: generosity, benevolence, compassion, willing to lend a helping hand, cooperation, respect for boundaries, aware of the power of life energy, healthy use of sexual energy. Concerning the latter: Taoist health trainer and teacher Mantak Chia has Nessus conjunct Sun opposition Hygeia!

My experience with Nessus transiting in hard aspect to the Sun is that this Centaur evokes an inner transformative crisis that demands clarity and decisive action based on "cut the crap". In the personal horoscope Nessus can be a player with violent impact. *Forcing entry* seems to be the core quality of this Centaur. In harmonious aspects, this gaining access goes pretty easy, while in hard aspects, where access is denied, it has to be forced open and in extreme cases violence is used. Thus, in line with these characteristics, Nessus also has to do with breakthrough, breakout, escape, rescue and hacking. Computer hacking is a Nessus-thing pur sang, especially when combined with Mercury, Uranus, Vesta or Makemake. Also espionage, spies, officers, burglars, rapists, rape in general – mentally or emotionally – black magic, executioners, cracking a closed system (be it a nut or oyster or bank vault, or mind frame), assassins and police raid teams reside under Nessus.

The centaur has an orbital period of 122 years and 153 days.

52872 OKYRHOE

Acceleration in general; psycho-synthesis in order to handle expansive career processes and harmonize them with the private life; to raise things, to reveal, uncover things, while this is not appreciated by everyone.

Okyrhoe was automatically discovered on September 19, 1998 by Spacewatch and measures 36 km in diameter. Okyrhoe means *running* or *fast-flowing.* The mythical Okyrhoe was the daughter of the centaur Chiron and the water nymph Chariklo. She had prophetic gifts and predicted the future of Aesculapius when he was a baby. She also revealed issues which the gods would have rather kept secret, for which she was punished by turning her into a mare.

Okyrhoe was discovered in conjunction with the star 51 Pegassi in the constellation Pegasus, the flying horse of Bellerophon, at 24°35 Pisces opposition her discovery-Sun at 26°08 Virgo. Like all celestial bodies found with their own discovery position in the sign opposite to the sign in which their discovery-Sun is placed Okyrhoe is gifted with a strong ambition eager to assert its talents publicly. We see this demonstrated in Eris, Bienor, Typhon, Circe and many more newcomers.

In case of strong oppositions within just 2 degrees or 1 degree (like Bienor) the urge to reach the top is very dominant, which however does not necessarily mean that the energy expresses itself in a Saturn or Pluto-like endeavor for status or power. Yet, there is always a desire to come into the limelight, or to step into the Sun-light, as it were. However, in the case of Okyrhoe it all becomes a bit more complex as its Sun is in the 4th house, the house that rules our private life. Okyrhoe is conjunct Gorgo (*relationship crisis*) / 1999 TC36 (*metaphysics and to summarize complexities in simple terms*) / Jupiter (*expansion*) in Pisces, where Jupiter is strong, yet distorted in conjunction with 2003 WL7 (*abrupt, explosive*). The Sun is conjunct Amun (*ambition*) / Lachesis (*stop a process*) / 2001 FL194 (*Plutonian intensity*) and Thisbe (*suicidality*). Sun and Okyrhoe make sextiles and trines to the axis 2nd house 8th house from a complex 4th house – 10th house entanglement.

Another striking feature in the discovery chart of Okyrhoe is that Mercury in Virgo and Mars in Leo are both making very narrow aspects with a whole series of Centaurs and Plutinos, by which they are therefore stimulated strongly, while positioned in a rough halfsextile. This results in a situation wherein the nourishing aspects to Mercury act as the hard aspects to Mars and vice versa. In plain English: *this gives much dissonance between thought and action*. As all Centaurs more or less emit some kind of dissonance, this conflict between thought and action distinguishes Okyrhoe in this aspect. The North nodes are conjunct, but one is in Virgo and the other in Leo; yet together they are in the third house. Thus Okyrhoe's destiny within all this complexity is to shine, through excellent communication and research. Moon in Virgo conjunct Echeclus underlines the communication element.

The interpretation then points to: the balancing of ambition/career/aspirations with the home environment/private life; to create and stabilize financial means; a sudden change of the course of life through a relationship crisis; the pursuit towards clarity and the concrete, from states that are vague, woolly or passive; a sudden acceleration of the expansion drive, beginning with some kind of popping entry (like writing a successful debut by which your career gets a major boost); the need to create an enduring synergy between doing and thinking and regular setbacks as long as this synergy has not yet been achieved; to become aware of obstructive thought and do-patters; to gain or lose one's popularity; the risk of the loss of one's family or home or financial basis and the need for psycho-synthesis (classic Virgo affliction problem).

Finally Okyrhoe points at the risk of nervous breakdowns and intestinal problems, heart problems or foot problems when a given project increases or evolves so fast that one loses control over it. In such cases the usual scenario is that the project is discontinued due to health reasons, third parties, or financial setbacks, and even bankruptcy is possible. Psycho-synthesis and keeping the balance between private needs and career demands are important things with Okyrhoe. A tough Centaur to curb, but, once understood, an uplifting force and robust motor. The Neptune square to Black Moon in the discovery chart indicates purge processes concerning the visionary aspect of Okyrhoe, which, as will be clear by now, parallels the main lesson to be learned from this Centaur.

In a weak and negative chart Okyrhoes' lessons are not learned, and, as a result, it are always the others or the situations that are blamed for one's own time-consuming and costly failures. And again, without seat-belts, one goes for another roller-coaster ride until the forces invoked will catapult someone directly out into the blue. Okyrhoe can be especially problematic in Fire and Air signs, because there is already a lot more acceleration than in Water and Earth.

The orbital period is 24 years and 108 days.

330836 ORIUS

Social intelligence; passionate freedom-loving and liberating; freedom associated with Age of Aquarius-like views on love and living together; the introduction of the new in the old, after having screened the old on outdated and faulty aspects; mocking politics; cannot take the old political system and authority seriously; inconsistencies in views or activities; presents the crooked or immoral as straight or justified; being ruthless or hard; technical talents; a tendency to screening.

Orius measures about 46 km across and was discovered on April 25, 2009 by Kazimieras Černis. Orius was conjunct the star Princeps (*happiness but problems, discontent and fear caused by one's own audacity instead of conditions*) in the 4th degree Scorpio sextile Pluto/1994 JR1 in Capricorn. The name Orius means *of the mountain* and can be traced in different Greek myths. In one, he is a centaur being slain by Heracles, in another a mountain god.

More appropriate for the astrological analogy is the myth of a monstrous giant with enormous powers, who lived in the Thracian wilderness, half-human-half-bear, with cannibalistic behavior and no respect for the laws of the gods (authorities). As punishment for their disobedience this Orius (Oreios) and his twin brother Agrios (meaning *Wild*, or *Savage one*) were changed into a vulture and an eagle owl by the god Hermes. Paradoxically it was never really expected that the brothers would obey the gods. Their mother was Polyphonte, who irritated the goddess Aphrodite because she did not worship her. Out of sheer annoyance she made Polyphonte fall madly in love with a bear, with which she mated, thus receiving her children Oreios and Agrios as half human, half bear. To make it worse, the Goddess Artemis was so disgusted by this, that she sent all her wild animals at Polyphonte to make her constantly live in fear.

For decades Orius was in close conjunction (usually within 1 degree) with 2003 CO1; the conjunction being exact during the heydays of the hippie era. Orius has two faces. First, there is the Orius who has social intelligence and is a passionate lover of freedom and liberation. This Orius is especially associated with Age of Aquarius-like views on love and living together; introducing the new into the old, after having screened the old on outdated and faulty aspects. In line with this are features like: the anti-authoritarian humanist who mocks politics and refuses to see the old or ruling political system as a natural or intelligent social environment (Pallas conjunct Kwak in discovery chart); vague "spiritual" individual relationships, or the opposite: a really deep relationship with the partner; being tolerant; persistent and consistent in the alternative; inspiration and the creative vibe.

On the other hand and in contrast to the qualities mentioned above, Orius can manifest a hard, ruthless nature, even express itself violently and sometimes there is a technical talent or a tendency towards screening. However, this rarely prevails. Rather we see contrasting views or opinions on a topic or activity in one and the same person. Orius has thus a relation with being inconsistent in one's opinions or creating a huge contrast between ones personal or corporate image and ones true nature or crooked methods. One's fans or public may also react this way. This feature is prominent in the chart of Steve Jobs and flanked by his Bienor-aspectation. Jobs was idolized as a groundbreaking innovator and even a messiah, but his company Apple was founded on outrageous exploitation of poor miners and Chinese factory workers, serious environmental pollution and government backed distorted safety regulations for the use of wireless devices. The scandals and inhumane aspects of Apple even inspired documentary makers.

Steve Jobs had Orius in conjunction Moon / Eris / 2003CO1 / Pandora sextile 1992QB1 / Damocles; square Lilith (*children exposed to severe cancer-causing radiation on iPad-schools*). Bill Gates (Pizza Gate, environmental scandals, accused of damaging ten thousands of children in India with vaccines), has Orius conjunct Eris / 2003CO1; trine Echeclus ; square 1993 SC / Icarus / Pest; square Minerva; opposition Hebe; sextile 1996 TO66. Udo Ulfkotte (first a follower of mainstream journalism, later whistleblower on the CIA infiltrating European news agencies) had Orius opposition Moon and square Salacia. Julian Assange has Orius conjunct 2003 CO1 opposition Moon; square Asbolus / Hopi / Orpheus / Dionysus; square 1998 SM165; trine 1996 GQ21 (Virgo) and 1 minute exact trine 2005 RN43 (Capricorn). According to Philip Sedgwick, Orius especially relates to the balance of values and professional and personal relationships.

The orbital period is 98 years and 354 days.

49036 PELION

Healing or recreating one's own will, to merge this will with one's true aspiration into unstoppable and passionate ambition and to become famous quite suddenly as a result of this inner process; the crystallization of willpower; what turns out to be someone's real aspiration and the way one wants to be seen by others; many fears in the first part of life; late bloomers.

Pelion was discovered on August 21, 1998 by Robert Whiteley and David Tholen. Just like in the discovery-charts of Bienor and Okyrhoe, Pelion was in the sign opposite the sign where the Sun was located – indicating a desire to be at the top of something somewhere or to achieve something that becomes known to a wider audience. Sun, Moon, Mercury, Venus and Mars are in Leo, so this sign has a dominant influence over this Centaur. Pelion wants to shine and be the center of attention, but experiences a wound concerning its willpower. Saturn on the cusp of the 11th house frustrates the creative 5th house – 11th house axis-dynamics. Pluto is conjunct Hidalgo, which causes the willpower (Pluto) to burst apart, as it were. This weakening of will-focus is pushed even further by the uncorrected Black Moon in Scorpio., which emphasizes "process" at the cost of any stable factor in life.

Key concepts of Pelion are: development, the fine tuning of willpower; what your real aspiration is and how it will harmonize with the way other people perceive you, even after you passed away; how you want to be seen by others; the activation of an inexhaustible source of aspiration and ambition once your true, natural will has been recognized and focused.

In some horoscopes Pelion acts as an incentive for homosexuality, or more generally for taking the passive role when having anal sex, or a love for anal masturbation. Pelion also has a strong connection with the 3rd house 9th house-axis, with its discovery-Sun conjunct cusp 3 in Leo, adding a creative component to the axis of communication, information and travel/transport. During the process in which ones true will emerges from the blurred version one has mistakenly pursued so long, one will encounter many distractions and delays that require self integrity as a mental, emotional, spiritual "lubricant". In the early part of life, people with a dominant Pelion in their birth chart usually have to overcome many fears or phobias, that block the entrance to a full dynamic life. Once the healing of the wounded will is solidified, the true will can emerge with a tremendous power and expansive drive, often accompanied by a now or never realism and fatalism, mirrored in the age one has reached (Varuna conjunct Ascendant / Apophis) as the Pelion-true-will-discovery-process can easily absorb one third or even half of one's life. It is not uncommon for Pelion's 'ripening' to be catalyzed by the return of Chiron, when the 51st birthday is approaching.

In comparison to Hylonome, which can raise even very young people to world-wide popularity and Bienor, which brings the fame usually in the early midlife period, a strong Pelion gives its reward usually in the second half of one's life.

Pelion's raw uncut, intrinsic energy is expressed at its strongest and purest through the mind of (homosexual) authors with a preference for the decadent, erotic and / or gothic genre. Oscar Wilde had Pelion in Gemini in the 10th house trine Makemake / Vertex (*The Picture of Dorian Grey* is based on a biohack principle: a precursor of Makemake's transhumanism); sextile 1998 HK151 (*word power*); opposition Icarus (*stream of inspiration*) and 2001 XA255 (*to be persecuted*).

The orbital period of Pelion is 89 years and 135 days.

5145 PHOLUS

The sudden inspired undermining of a stable situation; ideas, information, "hunches" suspicions popping up at irregular intervals within an environment that is experienced as dissonant with one's own being; vague intuitions that turn out to be correct after all, combined with a lack of organizational skills; getting into the position of a side-liner, against all odds; having the feeling of being driven or pushed towards something while the reason is not clear; to perceive the comical side of misfortune and tragedy; landslides; liquid light.

Pholus is a Saturn, Uranus and Orcus crossing Centaur, discovered on January 9, 1992, either automated by Spacewatch or (not officially recognized) by David Lincoln Rabinowitz. The composition of this Centaur is complex and contains olivine, ice, methanol ice and especially many carbon compounds which give Pholus its dark surface. Pholus measures 190 km in diameter. The name Pholus comes from the Greek word Φωλος derived from *phôleos*, meaning *"from the cave"*.

Pholus, like Chiron, was civilized, and indeed – in art – sometimes shared the "human-centaur" features by which Chiron was sometimes depicted (that is, he was a man from head to toe, but with the center and rear parts of a horse attached to his buttocks). This form was used to differentiate Chiron and Pholus from all other centaurs, who were mostly represented as men only from the head to the waist, and therefore more animal-like. Though there are other mythical versions, Pholus accidentally wounded and poisoned himself with one of Heracles' venomous arrows and died as a result.

The discovery chart of Pholus shows a most peculiar supersatellitium in Capricorn consisting of a conjunction Scientia / Chrisodom / Sun / Hilda / Split / Neptune / Uranus / Damocles. It is square Eris / Pandora; square Deucalion and opposition Solidarity / Sila Nunam. The discovery position of Pholus itself is 00°36 Leo in the 9th house opposition Black Moon in Capricorn. The cusp of the 9th house is conjunct Chariklo. The discovery-ascendant in the 6th degree of Scorpion conjunct the "NLP Plutino" 1998 HK151; square Saturn trine Chariklo. Nessus is conjunct Rhiphonos in Libra trine Vertex and Crantor opposition Juno.

A dominant Pholus in the natal chart, channels, at irregular intervals, ideas, information, "hunches", suspicions within an environment that is characterized as a settled or closed system, while a chronic dissonance is experienced between this system and one's own being.

Pholus links progress and improvement with the spontaneous and intuitive, and although many of Pholus' vague intuitions turn out to be true afterwards and reveal something essential, Pholus usually misses the constructive ability and organizing forces to turn this gift into something useful. Thus Pholus remains a sideliner within the evolutionary developments of society – something Pholus abhors. This Centaur thus disrupts the orderly system of belief or routine, and sometimes just throws things apart. Pholus is therefore associated by some astrologers with the first domino stone to fall or with the butterfly effect.

Within the relational field and in terms of contracts, treaties, alliances, Pholus can be pretty disastrous. Pholus' real work consists of purging the qualities and situations of (outdated) conservatisms which resort under the sign of Capricorn and its ruler Saturn. It does so despite a tendency of the Pholian type of person to simply treat these energies and psycho-spheres with cynical humor. The most suitable media for the Pholus-type for expressing his or her energy are language and writing, although they should educate themselves on the effects of language and its NLP-aspect, if they want to be taken seriously. Also recommended is cultivating one's own antenna for sensitive, psychic or paranormal impressions. Initially there is a lot of confusion here, but focused study and proper guidance can bring something of value to the surface. The association with Pholus' escapist drink and drug use is highlighted in the discovery horoscope via the positions of Moon, Datura, and Bacchus.

Juan Antonio Revilla links Pholus to intelligence operations, orphans, scum, exodus, metamorphoses, invasion, cultural clashes, shamanism, the dispossessed, homeless people, torrential rain, waterfalls, Luciferian figures, vultures, incongruities, the butterfly and moth, a nomad, excitement and states of euphoria. Laurence Lucas associates Pholus with a reality meltdown, dissolving structures, *nothing is sacred*, the *spiritual hypermarket*, a surreal atmosphere, liquid light and the future as the past. Dieter Koch and Robert von Heeren link Pholus to: Unlived, underdeveloped and latent personality parts are activated and driven to incarnation (disinhibition). The old and formerly protective, but too narrow life form which is often removed unusually easily and quickly (moulting and liberation). The need for further development and change coming to the surface. Learning to unfol d new strengths through excessive demands and great challenges. Something that is integrated into one's own being that was previously inaccessible or alien to it and was therefore rejected. Protective barriers which are lifted in borderline situations. The danger of self-sabotage and loss of control. Leaving the old structure through spontaneous awareness of problems, mistakes, deficiencies and deficits. Von Heeren also mentions the thin line between madness and genius as a Pholus feature. Godwin Cooke adds to Pholus: extreme development at the cost of the inner order or structure and cohesion and extreme development of something at the cost of quality and refinement, putting quantity above quality.

The orbital period of Pholus is 91 years and 176 days.

1994 TA PYLENOR

To escape into alcohol or drugs; a "tunnel feeling" instead of a tunnel vision, the urge to get out of a certain situation or condition; energies or persons who unwittingly enter the private sphere; forced fusions; the search for freedom in the private sphere; hedonism; healing through poison or self purging; toughness; a complex emotional life; to end up in the gutter, emotionally, socially and/or financially; empathy; artistic talent; fermentation, decay, putrefaction.

Pylenor is the unofficial, but widely accepted name for 1994 TA. The Centaur has no MPC number yet (while producing this book). The object was discovered on October 2, 1994 (the JPL small body database does not provide information about the discoverer) in the 19th degree Aries conjunct Eris / Leviathan; square Ate; sextile Okyrhoe; opposition Deucalion. The diameter is estimated at 30 km. Allthough1994 TA has not received any number of the MPC, *Robert von Heeren* published the *7- Centaur Ephemeris*, containing the data of Pylenor.

Features: dealing with some sort of invasion or forced fusion; hedonism; healing through poison or self purging; a flight into alcohol or drugs; toughness; the search for freedom in the private sphere; to live at the edge of society or in the gutter; a complex emotional life; the feeling of being trapped in yourself and seeking a way out by mystical means or by proper cognitive methods, processes or therapies. The results are generally unsatisfactory because the Moon in the discovery chart of Pylenor is at the epicenter of a dichotomy between the ultra rational and extremely spiritual (Moon conjunct Logos / Hypnos in the 3th degree Virgo = Midpoint Varuna/ Typhon on the cusp 12 | Rhiphonos / Urhixidur / Mercury in five (in Scorpio). Rather than suffering from a tunnel vision, someone with a strong Pylenor sits trapped in what you could describe as a "tunnel feeling".

The feeling is just as intense as it is rigid, as Virgo and the Logos/Hypnos conjunction are able to sedate it, but especially Typhon (*keep on the infighting!*) and Rhiphonos (*get rid of the man or mouse-dilemna!*) keep pushing. This is flanked by the conjunction Thereus / North node /Jupiter / Venus / Nessus in 4 in Scorpio which craves for an intense, unrestrained feeling of happiness based on the intimate and one's self-integrity. Pylenor has related itself to a desire for pleasure and luxury, and complex and obscure processes that build up bad karma based on ancestry or family history. In contrast, Pylenor's force under control makes extremely sharp, analytical and investigative.

The inner world is extremely active compared to its involvement with the outside world. Subjective reality is prevailed over the objective; the intense is more attractive than the convivial. Pylenor has a dark, dramatic side that has everything to do with the very compelling position of the SDO 1999 TD10 (*invasions, forced fusions*). This SDO, strong in Aquarius, inconjuncts Moon; opposes the Leo-Ascendant and squares Rhiphonos. In addition to the inwardly directed forces of Scorpio, Pylenor is impregnated with the invasion theme, being forced to resist invasion or purging these sort of conditions. House, sign and aspects of Pylenor in the Natal, Progressed or Solar chart indicate how and in what area of your life, what kind of intruder or unauthorized and unwanted intrusion, or fusion or alliance may be expected.

In the first house Pylenor will, when afflicted, usually manifest as some sort of invasion of the body like a wound, insect bite, viral or bacterial infection, poisoning, or in extreme cases becoming the unsolicited victim of donor organ removal, etc.. In the second house your financial security, possessions or talent may be ruined by a third party; in the 3rd house one can expect a lot of trouble from neighbors, brothers or sisters who behave parasitical or do not respect your private space or life ambitions, or you may suffer from a traffic accident caused by someone else – most likely by a drunk or a drug user. In four the invasion manifests itself in your home or in the first or last period of your life. In the 4th house Pylenors influence can take many forms. Circumstances, such as for instance a psychiatric condition of one of the parents may change a feeling of being at home and safe into a chronic threat. You house may become the target of burglars, an epicenter of paranormal activity, like a haunting, ley-line vortex or other negative energetic disposition. With Aquarius or Uranus on the cusp of the 4th house you may suffer from an insane high level of electro-smog from nearby transmission towers or excessive wifi from your neighbors. As a child you could suffer from a psycho-energetic form of extortion. In 5, caring for children can become someone's breaking point, for example because of ADHD, or some other condition which absorbs almost all your energy. Pylenor can also express itself in 5 as an unbalanced sex life (rape within marriage, invasive power-plays, bizarre perversions). Also the side effects of a gambling addiction gone out of hand may invade your life, or some creative idea or work you produced is stolen or damaged. In 6 Pylenor can give very unpleasant situations at work or one is pulled out of one's routine due to badly timed health problems. In 6 Pylenor makes a person more susceptible to viral diseases and infections and the daily work situation or health in general can suck too much energy. In the 7th house two partners will be tested by something or someone's attempt to put a wedge between the two partners; In the 8th house one may expect an invasion by the IRS or get bad investments forced upon you, or problems on the occult plane, such as problems with the spirits of the deceased or black magic. Sexual exhaustion from porn or masturbation-addiction is another option. In the 9th house a philosophy or belief can be forced upon you and trading companies that export abroad can be forced into unwanted fusions. Far abroad and in dreams you may have strange experiences. In 10 your career may suffer either from your own behavior or a third party. Pylenor in 11 attracts parasitic or drug or alcohol addicted friends or one may suffer from the rules and demands of a political or cultural group that overrules your personal reality and needs. In 12, the drugs and booze link that Pylenor has, will most likely be underlined while Pylenor in 12 can easily trigger and catalyze the self-undoing aspect of the 12th house.

Unlike 1999 TD10, which, in terms of invasion and forced fusions, shows a large overlap with Pylenor, this Centaur does not react in an extrovert and pro-active way to invasion (fight back, get stronger, create a kind of empire; the empowerment of one's own activities through expansion strategies and the better constructing of one's own activities, ambition and securing the aspiration and creative flow). Instead, Pylenors first reaction is to *implode*, purging all emotional and cognitive data, or using stimulants/sedatives like alcohol or drugs. With a strongly afflicted and dominating Pylenor, the simple pressure from the everyday rat race is usually enough to use these resources, to "numb" the "invasion aspect", and paradoxically, by doing so, regain control.

The North node in Scorpio conjunct Thereus/Venus/Jupiter/Nessus effectuates this contra-reaction as long as someone with a dominant Pylenor understands that the counter-reaction is a form of invasion by itself, and realizes that what one really wants is to simply feel comfortable and free within the private sphere. As long as this insight remains absent the afflicted Pylenor-type usually remains trapped in a vicious cycle of invasion and counter-reaction, feeding two negative currents at the same time, making this person alienate more and more from his or her own live. Thus Pylenor is portrayed as very negative by most astrologers. The reason is, of course, that if the Pylenor-type gets stuck in this loop, it inevitably ends up destructive, with indeed all Pylenor clichés as drug or alcohol addiction, self-poisoning, poisoning the social environment, polluting oneself, venereal diseases, AIDS, neglect, festering wounds, etc.. The whole palette that you can find in the gutter among the homeless and addicted.

Zane B. Stein however correctly associated Pylenor also with the creation of antibodies and the use of small amounts of poison in order to promote healing. In this respect Pylenor has a theoretical link with homeopathy, ayahuasca or psylocibine sessions, the use of oxygen therapy via MMS or hydrogen peroxide. Products that are the result of fermentation fall under Pylenor. Also exhausting activities or habits, the tapping of liquids and the rotting process are a Pylenor-matter. Another positive aspect of Pylenor lies in the potential of being able to surrender to a total, orgiasmic enjoyment of special/exalted states of mind and feeling, whereby all influences of the rat race or whatever obligations one accumulates as an adult, are absent and whereby these states are induced by drugs, sex, alcohol or whatever other stimulant/sedative one prefers to use. In our modern Christianity and pragmatism based society the importance of what Swami Beyondananda called "mental floss" is denied or commercialized by Big Pharma and cloaked by social media addiction. Because of this, the modern way of life has become so stuffed with frustration that frustration became "institutionalized" and its very smoldering, rotten basis. Life itself is no longer directly felt or experienced, but analyzed, cataloged, sterilized, politisized, lied about, automatically piloted and destroyed because of financial interests, in fact, a diapositive of true civilization is distorting our natural urge to experience happiness, and this mudstream touches everyone.

From a social perspective negative Pylenor-types are characterized by claiming attention and energy from others, misusing their own misery, addiction, disease or physical condition. They also manifest a very "ambivalent" relationship with lies. The invasion is, as it were, reversed, and projected on the other, resulting in a convulsion instead of a solution. Yet, despite all the misery mentioned above, this Centaur can manifest its energy in a totally different and mature way. The positive Pylenor is actually very aware of all the shit and problems associated with this rather radical Centaur on an intuitive level and therefore capable of great empathy and understanding. One can therefore do very well as a social worker, actor, artist or author. Researcher Zane B. Stein published a series of celebrities (actors and authors) with strong Pylenor conjunctions in the natal chart, including Marlon Brando, Dennis Hopper, Katharine Hepburn, Leonardo di Caprio, Deborah Harry, Marcel Duchamp, Honoré de Balzac and Herman Melville. Talents that would have achieved nothing without their deep understanding of human drama. The positive Pylenor-type is a great go-getter. In research work they dig right to the bottom, thus adding some bright colors at the predominantly dark aura of this complex Centaur.

The orbital period of Pylenor is 68 years and 146 days.

346889 RHIPHONOS

Man or mouse issues; passion as proofreader; animating a stalled ambition or project; God helps the brave; the freedom-shaping qualities of music of the Air-element.

Rhiphonos was discovered on August 28, 2009 by T.V. Kryachko and measures 23.20 km in diameter. During its discovery Riphonos was in the 17th degree Aries which has an intrinsic connection with the Air element, Air elementals and music. It was conjunct the Plutino 1995 QY9 (*passion, all or nothing*). The trine Pluto-Orcus in the discovery chart is almost minute exact and responsible for the fatalistic now or never-thing, which is Rhiphonos' main feature. Sun is conjunct Zephyr and Venus is conjunct the asteroid Spirit. In most situations Rhiphonos has to do with a courage test annex (self) integrity test. Transits from Rhiphonos to important planets or points in the radix horoscope invariably revolve around a situation in which one has to ask the well-known question “I am a man or a mouse?”.

Rhiphonos learns to *rediscover* his own passion and points out that ambitions, aspirations and passion must be synchronised if our course is to be the right one and the path of our heart. In the Rhiphonian process there is at first a notion of being stuck or an impasse, then an awareness of a farce, dead end or dormant state or wrong turn that was taken earlier in life, followed by the decision to take the leap to another course, another attitude, by means of which a different actuality, life situation and future (perspective) is created. In most cases it’s all a matter of perspective how one shapes one’s future.

Rhiphonos either brings a refreshing, liberating energy for those who believe in the old credo “God helps the brave” or a shameful and weak moment for those who are afraid and let a good opportunity to change their live for the better pass – often with severe consequences in later life like a smoldering feeling of shame over one’s own cowardice that permanently poisons one’s own remaining life or that of others and perhaps even worse: missing the very goal and essence of one’s current incarnation. The Air-element, passion and energy of Rhiphonos helps us to escape from an impasse by making us realize its laming effect on our lives and simultaneously this Centaur shows us the new horizon. There are several asteroids that should never be left out of a chart interpretation of a client if the astrologer wants to present him or her with an advise that is really substantial. Rhiphonos is certainly one of them, as the fundamental meaning of life is to *thrive* and become this unique flower in the great field of flowers, your heart knows, but your mind and the environment do so often deny or obstruct. Step into the Sun!
Finally I want to emphasize the fact that *the size of an asteroid does not necessarily equal its importance!*

The orbital period of Rhiphonos is 35 years and 190 days.

32532 THEREUS

A rutting animal; Satyr energy; expressionism; the caged animal that wants out, the pressure of caged emotions and instincts, outbursts; potency, phallic energy, enormous creative, sexual or physical strength that is difficult to manage or has trouble finding a way out; conflicts between instincts and social codes, collisions with authorities, control systems and control freaks; a bond with Elemental forces; voodoo drums; duende, Flamenco, absorbs the energy of the Earth through the soles of the feet; dangerous if challenged or attacked; hates or dislikes technology, weak in technical abilities, dis-calculi, a predisposition to spelling mistakes; putting content above form, an aversion to formalities; physical characteristics that have something animal like, a great love for wild nature, untouched forests; having a magical bond with animals; big appetite; Sylvanus, Basajaun, wild men, woodwose; the art of staying pure and natural.

Thereus was discovered on August 9, 2001 by Near Earth Asteroid Tracking (NEAT) and named after the mythical hunter Thereus, famous for catching bears and dragging them alive, and very pissed off, to his cave. The orbit of this Centaur crosses that of Saturn and Jupiter. A strongly placed Thereus in the natal chart can be characterized with the following descriptions: raw explosive animal energy, the caged beast that wants out, the pressure of caged emotions and instincts, schizophrenia, borderline, eruptions; potency, phallic energy, enormous creative, sexual or physical strength that is difficult to manage or has trouble finding a way out; conflicts between instincts and social codes, collisions with authorities, control systems and control freaks, rut, rutting animals, great sex drive, satyr nature, lustful, sexual; bond with Elemental forces; voodoo drums, African drumming and dancing, hardcore punk or metal; duende, Flamenco, absorbs the energy of the Earth through the soles of the feet, virile power, survival talent, wildness, fury, dangerous if challenged or attacked; hates technology, weak in technical abilities, dis-calculi, predisposition to spelling mistakes; putting content above form, aversion to formalities or disrupting them; physical characteristics that have something animal like, great love for wild nature, untouched forests and animals versus pollution and environmental destruction; aversion to animal cruelty; a strange magical bond with animals which is confirmed by others who witness this feature; anti-civilization; affinity with primitive / natural people; animism; tragic or violent experiences where it concerns love and the heart; lust for life; hunger; big appetite; third chakra problems; overactive lower chakras, Kundalini power; aversion to spiritual mumbo jumbo and state religions; passion as a religious experience, God = Nature; Tarzan, Basajaun, Sylvanus, wild men, woodwose; expressionism; intemperance; the art of staying pure, real and natural. Finally, invocation (voluntary possession) of nature spirits associated with power or sex is rather easy with a strong Thereus in the birth chart.

Thereus tends to vegetarianism, but remains a meat eater out of physical (protein) needs. Cultivation and everything that has to do with cultivation is Thereus' personal problem zone. Thereus is *intrinsically uncultivated*, but despite this precondition this force wants to learn to express itself through especially the Mercurial way (Mercury conjunct North nodes in the discovery horoscope) and is forced to do so by the social environment. The energy of Thereus is so turbulent and direct that its great creative potential is very difficult to channel through the more technical media. Because Thereus' core identity *is* the impetuous self, it soon feels like loss of identity if its wildness is encapsulated for any purpose and this actually gives a chronic dormant conflict between the animal and over-cultivated human nature in both the psyche and the instinctual life. Thereus is the original expressionist.

Suppression of Thereus' energy can lead to severe psychological and psychosomatic problems, even of the genre that can evoke a psychoses. Thereus in Capricorn, Libra or Virgo quickly leads to this repression. Conversely, however, Thereus in Leo, Aries, Sagittarius and Scorpio may stimulate the worst part of their alter egos. Almost every non-natural system gets on Thereus' nerves and feels like a chain around the neck. *Punk never dies* in Thereus' brain. When the energy flourishes within civilized channels, Thereus still maintains a rawness and wildness, in the sense that he does not care much how its own actions or visions collide with any kind of consensus, image, cultural mind frame or expectation pattern – thus creating a typical bad boy aura.

Quoting Heath Letchers words through the mouth of the Joker: *I'm not a planner. Just do things...* Letcher, in addition to his Sun/Silly conjunction, had Thereus square Mars/Lachesis (*endings by action or violence*); trine Damocles/BAM (*abruptly disturbing the order*); trine Elatus; sextile Rhadamantus (*law*); opposition 1999 XX143 (*provocation*), and gave the Joker, at the time already an often ruminated figure, with this mix, a power, which resulted in one of the most impressive acting achievements in film history, ever.

Where Thereus' energy is harnessed within the creative, it is impossible to characterize the outcome better than with this quotation from John Cowper Powys: '*... that formidable daimon, which... can be reached somewhere in my nature, and which when it is reached has the Devils own force. ...I became aware more vividly than I had ever been, that the secret of life consists in sharing the madness of God, I mean the power of rousing a peculiar exultation in yourself as you confront the Inanimate, an exultation which is really a cosmic eroticism.*'

Aware of the raw nature versus civilization conflict, Thereus can express this energy in some horoscopes as a coarse sense of humor or spicy cultural philosophical writings and discussions. Moreover, Thereus is strongly represented in the sex industry, which is still seen as a the collapse of civilization by those people endowed with a talent for civilian hypocrisy. The latter is a Plutonic element within this Centaur: the confrontation with the denied or repressed instinct. Because of the rawness, Thereus' energy is more often expressed through sex or porn than art (a very tight Venus/Bacchus/Elatus opposition Pluto in the discovery-horoscope). In radix horoscopes Thereus is usually the most expressive via contacts with Sun, Ruler, Ascendant or Moon. The restless Dutch filmmaker and interviewer Theo van Gogh (notorious for his ill-mannered directness) and Courtney Love (angry vagina-rock bitch) both have a strong Thereus-Moon aspect. Actor Idris Elba has Sun in Virgo trine Thereus in Taurus and often plays a role in which he uses a lot of brute force against his opponents, literally throwing or dragging them wherever he (the director) wants them.

The orbital period of Thereus is 34 years and 289 days.

CENTAURS WITH A CODE NAME AND MPC-NUMBER, NOT OFFICIALLY NAMED YET

33128 1998 BU48 (NAME SUGGESTION: BIM)

Attracting money, wealth, the incitement of a money flow (income) and the possibilities this gives you; the power of money, capitalist thinking, money-related pragmatism, an unhealthy dependence of the self-esteem on money and a rather arrogant attitude towards dissidents in that area; financial worries; the development of talents.

1998 BU48 is a large centaur of 213 km in diameter – sometimes classified as a quasi-centaur or Kuiper-belt SDO. It was discovered on January 22, 1998 by Nichole M. Danzl. 1998 BU48 is primarily about money. When there are no big spoilers running at the same time, like a square Saturn – Jupiter or something, especially the positive aspects, like a trine to your radix-Sun, will usually manifest themselves in a very beneficial way as far as your income is concerned. Either direct or via fortunate business plans which will bear fruit later. 1998 BU48 is a very suitable Centaur to use in financial horoscopes or for making astro-magical amulets according to the Picatrix method. Matches well

with Jupiter, Varuna, Fortuna, Abundantia, Midas and 2001 BL41.
1998 BU48 is one of the most influential bodies of this time since on July 4, 1776, it made an exact trine with the US-ascendant from 12°13 Aries in the 4th house to the US-ascendant in 12°28 Sagittarius. Under the dominion of a psychopath, pushy and destructive Mars in 7 in Gemini – under the influence of 2011 WU92 (*extreme persuasion*) – these two Centaurs give the US its ferocious capitalistic base. The nature of 1998 BU48 corresponds to the energy of Jupiter in Taurus in the second house. It rules the attraction of money, wealth, the incitement of a money flow (*income*) and the possibilities this brings into your life. In a negative sense: the power of money, capitalist thinking, money-related pragmatism, the unhealthy dependence of the self-esteem on money and an arrogant attitude towards dissidents in that area and furthermore money worries if the Centaur does not get "attention", as it were. Allen Ginsberg, for example, had an almost minute exact sextile Moon – 1998 BU48. Money was a major stress factor in his life because of both his disinterest in, and his dependence on money. 1998 BU48 seems to dominate talents and can create a Wild West-like chaos from which the best and most useful options will be chosen. In the recent past, the Internet/World Wide Web went through such a phase. The disruptive effect of this Centaur obviously finds itself within the areas where identity and power (*abuse*) merge with wealth and money. Where every mature, intelligent person considers the dependence of self-esteem and status on property or money as the pinnacle of a plebs-mentality, it is the engine behind the lives of many who are internally unhappy, despite the successful decorum. A nation like the US itself, uses the oil-dollar link to extort the whole world, builds bubble constructions in the stock exchange world and is fully dependent on the weapon industrial cartel, media lies and endless series of very violent and murderous corporate wars, sponsored by banks. 1998 BU48 is challenging when money or capital seems to become identical with value, making us forget that value is only something we ourselves put onto something, and not an intrinsic quality. This also applies to gold.

The orbital period is 193 years and 68 days.

44594 1999 OX3

High sensitivity, very sensitive regarding relationship issues or communication with the partner; seeking a positive flow; integrity; predisposition to astrology and metaphysics; psychospheric intelligence; cynicism in frustration; resilience to stabilize quickly during a crisis situation.

1999 OX3 was discovered by J. J. Kavelaars, B. J. Gladman, M. J. Holman and J.M. Petit on July, 21 1999 and measures 192 km in diameter. The labeling of 1999 OX3 as a Centaur is controversial because the Minor Planet Center (MPC) and the Deep Ecliptic Survey (DES) use different criteria for the classification of an asteroid as a Centaur. DES labels 1999 OX3 as a Centaur. Therefore, in this book, it is classified as a (quasi-)Centaur, subject to future changes. 1999 OX3 is in the discovery chart in 2°41 Aquarius in the 11th house, conjunct Neptune and the Haumeid 1999 OY3 (*relationship issues*); square Jupiter in Taurus; trine Ceto in Libra. A strong 1999 OX3 can make one extremely sensitive in many different situations. There is even a prophetic instinct present that intuitively scans the future, a capacity to use the condition of the Zeitgeist of that moment as a kind of lens. 1999 OX3 gives trans-cognitive abilities and can translate intuitive and sensitive perceptions into understandable language; that is, if the high sensitivity does not turn into shyness and act as a brake on direct communication with others. In particular, 1999 OX3 is extremely sensitive within the relational sphere. The downside can be that one makes oneself inaccessible to the other with too much caution; gentlemen's/ladylike behavior, resulting in the other person unconsciously starting to mirror this behavior. Passion can than easily disappear from a relationship.

When 1999 OX3 positively addresses things, and this is badly received, this Centaur can unexpectedly express itself mercilessly sharp and cynical. This goes against the true nature of someone with a dominant 1999 OX3, because this person will always strive for a quick recovery of the harmony and peaceful dynamics in the relationship when having encountered a bump. 1999 OX3 gives, if the rest of the horoscope cooperates, a deep metaphysical insight and great talent for astrology. Sometimes there is a desire for a recreational or functional use of drugs. Although 1999 OX3 first manifests its energy through sensitivity, emotional intelligence, and intuition, the Centaur also increases cognitive abilities. Inherent and inevitable are frustrations that are encountered in society as a result of a quite radical out-of-the-box perception of reality. 1999 OX3 is pretty stubborn in a literal sense and therefore this Centaur has also been associated with street smartness. In the 6th house 1999 OX3 may give extreme physical reactions to what is sensitively picked up, as well as dramatic reactions and dangerous emotional fluctuations when a relationship crisis or quarrel presents itself. However, there is a great resilience, which has to do with the discovery-Ascendant in the first degree of Aries, which makes it possible to quickly recuperate mentally, so that one seldom fails completely as a result of intense emotional issues. This practical, pragmatic feature acts as a very welcome counterbalance to the overall sensitivity of 1999 OX3.

The orbital period is 181 years and 267 days.

63252 2001 BL41 (NAME SUGGESTION: CORNUCOPIA)

Abundance; beneficial for finances; modesty; liberation from sexual inhibitions; social and worldly involvement.

2001 BL41 measures 35 km in diameter and was automatically discovered on 19 January 2001 by Spacewatch. 2001 BL41 was in the discovery-chart conjunct the star Copula and Praamzius / Wurm / Midheaven in the 25th degree of Cancer; opposition Starr. This Centaur has both positively and negatively a strong preoccupation with the concept of abundance. In a positive sense, especially conjunct Sun, this can give the happy mindset that there are always enough financial resources, so that, as the direct result of this primarily unconscious attitude, money and resources are almost always abundant. If something strongly or traumatically interrupts this base attitude and belief, the influence reverses 180 degrees and one can get caught up in a continuous loss of money or livelihoods. I suggested Cornucopia (Horn of Abundance) for 2001 BL41 because this Centaur makes or can make you radically aware of what attracts or loses or rejects abundance. Peak experiences are possible in both directions. Mohandas Ghandi whose best-known portrait is that of a man, dressed only in a homemade loincloth behind a spinning wheel, had 2001 BL41 conjunct Arachne in Aquarius opposition Moon in Leo symbolizing the fact that the abundance can also consist of a great spirit – with the cotton spinning (Arachne) as a very interesting decor. 2001 BL41 also has a link with sexual development and exploration, setting a course (when activated) that should end in a full and totally guiltless enjoyment of sexual pleasures. Furthermore, in some horoscopes, the Centaur gives an increased social involvement, a sense of time, a certain tendency to erase oneself and a reluctance to receive deserved complimentary attention. Conjunct the Sun in a woman's horoscope 2001 BL41 may indicate the sudden unexpected death of the husband. 2001 BL41 can make a person very generous, especially when conjunct Sun, as I have seen in several cases. Willie Hutch (December 6, 1944 – September 19, 2005), an American soul singer, songwriter, record producer and recording artist for

the Motown record label during the 1970s and 1980s had this conjunction. His manager, Anthony Voyce, said of Hutch: "*I've never met a more generous and caring person.*"

The orbital period is 30 years and 183 days.

73480 2002 PN34 (NAME SUGGESTION PARASITE)

Parasitic issues; parasites; energy suckers; to depend on a "mask" or, on the contrary, unmasking; taking off the mask; being able to see through the sharp motives of others; great zest for work; aversion to bureaucracy; dependency issues; emotional instability and insecurity; an emotional life that seems cursed, or is tainted by others.

2002 PN34 was discovered automatically on 6 July 2002 by Near Earth Asteroid Tracking (NEAT). The Centaur – or quasi-Centaur – measures approximately 112 km in diameter. Keywords and concepts: dependency on a "mask", unmasking, taking off the mask, being able to see through the true motives of others razor-sharp; coming out for something or standing up for something; aversion to closed or unchanging systems; aversion to bureaucracy, administrative obligations, boring long-term routines and processes. 2002 PN34 also gives third chakra-like problems like independence – dependency issues and problems with setting the boundaries between what's yours or your private sphere and what belongs to the other. Also: emotional instability and insecurity; a life of feeling that seems cursed; chaos, being chaotic; dismantling or turning things upside down, problems with agreements; inertia because one feels disenfranchised, does not know where to start; great urge to express oneself verbally and/or creatively, problems with self-image and conceit; being trapped between the urge to act and the search for a channel or time to manifest the power to act; once very confident of oneself, one can manifest great zest for work, discipline and ingenuity; otherwise self-pity, stuck in mood swings, suicidal thoughts, parasitic behavior (by others or towards the other); martyr complexes.

Mark Andrew Holmes mentions the Jeanne d'Arc complex. What is still lacking is that 2002 PN34 seems to give a lot of hassle concerning women all the time, who, in a men's horoscope also substantially obstruct his work or consume everything that is earned without contributing anything (*parasitic relationships*). Laziness is also suggested as a feature of this Centaur, but I think it is not laziness, but rather inertia caused by unconsciously combining an overkill of directions and impulses with the problem of holding on to one's own identity per situation, so that one seems to be fluttering in all directions, resulting in a stalemate as a kind of survival mechanism. This Centaur has a lot of inherent activity and energy, but focus and perseverance are the big challenges. The best areas of expression for 2002 PN34 are the third and fifth house (*communication/writing and creativity/self-expression*), while, with a dominant 2002 PN34 in the birth-chart, the second and eighth house always seem to attract all the attention. The most difficult thing about this Centaur is that it is a heavy weight, who can suck a lot of energy from the other players in the horoscope, thus unbalancing the entire horoscopic construction. Therefore 2002 PN34 should be included in every personal horoscope reading. The house and sign-psychospheres in which 2002 PN34 appears are experienced every now and then (due to transits that activate 2002 PN34) as parasitic, and as problem zones which draw a disproportionate amount of energy. Conversely, the greatest work drive and inventiveness can also be manifested there. Mercury contacting the Centaur gives wonderful insights, but also a lot of hassle in the field of communication, whereby the cause lies outside yourself. This can take a lot of your energy and work and sometimes it seems you just have to wait until the aspect – the stirring up of 2002 PN34 – has passed. This transit can also bring a plague of flies into your home or make parasitic persons appear at the door or in your mailbox. In contacts with Mercury, Uranus or Neptune, extra vigilance is required with regard to hackers (*skimming, phishing and virus attacks*). Contacts – especially the conjunction is important – with other planets color the concept of parasitism each in their own way.

The orbital time is 172 years and 249 days.

87555 2000 QB243

Thoughtfulness; power issues around flaws in official information; blind spots in scientific or religious assumptions; major export cases and problems; controversies within the academic world; divorce lawyers; large travel and transport agencies.

2000 QB243 is considered to be a Centaur, quasi-Centaur and Scattered Disc Object (SDO). The best categorization is therefore actually that of Extended Centaur. 2000 QB243 was discovered by the Cerro Tololo Inter-American Observatory on 25 August 2000 and measures about 86 km in diameter. The interpretation seems to go in the direction of: thoroughly analyzing information before venting; thoughtfulness; power issues surrounding flaws in official information; a successful but often protracted fight for one's own income stream; elaborating raids or ideas very thoroughly before sharing or concreting them, after first having made the necessary blunders in this area; testing ideas and idealism with integrity criteria and loosening up what "one" thinks; a steadily growing and deepening of sexuality between two life partners.

More mundane/forensic: controversies within the academic world, conflicts between official truths or assumptions and journalistic reports; fake news issues; blind spots in scientific or religious assumptions; huge batches of exported goods that have to be returned en masse due to a defect (e.g. cars that are faulty) and become headlines in the newspapers; divorce lawyers; lawsuits following (large) (import/export) contracts; large travel and aviation organizations which can get into big trouble. The Thomas Cook Group that went bankrupt in September 2019, making headlines with over 600,000 travelers stranded worldwide, was founded as a fusion of the old Thomas Cook (since 1841) and MyTravel Group on June 19, 2007. I'm 200% certain they did not consult a qualified business-astrologer. The founding moment they choose could hardly have been worse, especially for this kind of business. Only a complete imbecile starts a traveling agency when Mercury is retrograde (no comments…) while Moon is conjunct Saturn in Leo and opposition Neptune in Aquarius (*total evaporation of a dignified profile, which took years to build*) and Sun opposition Pluto (*energy slurping power struggle shit*). That's for the conservative default astrologers; and they would have advised the CEO's to pick a better date. Even without knowing 2000 QB243 was in exact square to Jupiter and inconjunct Venus. By the way, the Retrograde Mercury was conjunct the asteroid Unsold – but that's just a bonus.

The orbital time of 2000 QB243 is 207 years and 4 days.

88269 2001 KF77 (NAME SUGGESTION: SHOUTER)

Grand proclamations, drawing attention; attention magnet; converting dissonance between "self-integrity" and "integrity" of society that is interwoven with self-confidence issues into a general story that "concerns everyone"; whistle-blowers; people who stir up the discussion fire; sharp brave investigative journalists or the proverbial elephants in the china cabinet, when making a lot of noise predominates over substantive arguments.

Centaur of about 55 km diameter, discovered on May 22, 2001 by M. W. Buie. 2001 KF77 was discovered in the 3rd degree Scorpio conjunct Hylonome square Black Moon in Aquarius. The discovery-Sun was in 2 Gemini conjunct the Plutino 1998 VG44 (*official state lies, disinformation*) / Sado (*can denote sadism or the theatrical*) / Wilson-Harrington (*future-oriented or contemporary, out of the box questions*) in exact opposition to Varda (*urge to make a heavy impact*) / Machiavelli (*power in charge*) in Sagittarius. Moon was in 28 Taurus opposition the Plutino 1998 HK51 (*word power, NLP*); square Pelion. Sun and Moon are in the 9th house. Mars is in the 3rd house conjunct Chiron (*blind spots*) opposition 2002 XU93 (*hyper-awareness, being destroyed by the forces of the prevailing mode of reality or chronically in conflict with it*) and inconjunct Moon. Moon is also in exact trine with 2002 PN34 in Capricorn, thus fed with issues of social parasitism within a conservative context or connotation. (often expressed by critics who use the Constitution to attack the strategies of New World Order-politicians and neoliberal CEO's.

The central drama of Centaur 2001 KF77 appears to be a dissonance between self integrity and the integrity of society and thus it seems to be interwoven with self-confidence issues. This often results in a Chiron-like media mission to make this dissonance structurally a public one instead of personal in order to force change. When 2001 KF77 is strongly aspected, there is certainly a passionate urge to expose social abuses. The way in which this is done is highly individual and diverse, with the notification that 2001 KF77, as this is often the case with Centaurs, has a high loose cannon level – even for a Centaur. Enfant terrible of the independent news circuit and human rights activist Alex Jones is an almost incarnate 2001 KF77. In his chart 2001 KF77 aspects the major character building blocks in his horoscope. His 2001 KF77 is in the 23th degree Leo opposition Sun / Damocles and sextile Moon; square MC / Apophis / Osiris and IC / Mars / Ceto. 2001 KF77 is conjunct Industria and trine 1999 OX3 / Klotho / Panacea. And of course, Alex Jones also has the conjunction Orius / 2003CO1, which acts as a catalyst on 2001 KF77, causing so much fear among the establishment, they cowardly sabotaged his website in cooperation with all the Internet giants. Whistleblower Edward Snowden has 2001 KF77 in the 11th degree Virgo conjunct Rhiphonos / Huya opposition 1993 SB/1993 SC; in almost minute exact square Mercury; trine Burney; trine Admetos; sextile Elatus / Psyche / Vulcanus; sextile Karma. Malcolm X, whose violent death in 1965 had a particularly strong influence on the Black Panther Movement, was born with 2002KF77 in the 23rd degree Taurus conjunct 2002 CX154/ Mjölnir / Empedocles trine Jupiter / Leopardi / Epops / 2002 VS2 (in Capricorn); trine Varda /Toro / Skepticus / Aunus (in Virgo); square Hybris; square Echeclus / Hebe / Circe / Anubis; sextile Hylonome and opposition Child. In the horoscope of the popular but skeptics-run, deformed and censored online encyclopedia *Wikipedia*, 2002 KF77 is conjunct Hylonome in Scorpio, in opposition Urania (*astrology*) and afflicted by a square Black Moon / Neptune / 1999 OX3. (With Skepticus conjunct Crantor / Midpoint

Orcus / Asbolus sextile Orcus and sextile Asbolus). Activist for natural and sustainable agriculture Vandana Shiva has 2001KF77 – beautifully symbolic – conjunct Persephone; trine Erda and sextile Sif / Armor. The Centaur is also trine Hidalgo; opposition Nietzsche / Discovery; square Fukushima and square Hexlein. Muammar Gadaffi had 2001 KF77 in Gemini conjunct Mercury / Atlantis / 2001 SQ73; trine Machiavelli; sextile 2001 XA255 / Kassandra; sextile Siva and square Photographica. Mohandas Ghandi had 2001 KF77 in the fourth degree Scorpio conjunct Mercury / Echeclus / Justitia / Anubis / Mjölnir; opposition Lachesis; trine Poor / 2001 SQ73 / Askalaphus; trine Admetos; square North node / Wild / Isis; sextile Chaos and sextile Beowulf / Hybris. In cases where the negative forces are dominating the horoscope, 2001 KF77 works the other way around, as in the charts of ethical whistleblowers. The psychopath and *Red Witch Hunt*-initiator Joseph McCarthy had the Centaur in exact trine with his Moon in Leo in 10 Sagittarius. The inherent drama of 2001 KF77 was deformed by his Sun and Mors-Sumnus-position and projected on innocent people.

The orbital period is about 133 years and 292 days.

95626 2002 GZ32

Pattern breaks; new perspectives that undermine or render obsolete the validity of the old; sensing errors or blind spots in routines, habits, assumptions and systems or processes, no matter how firmly rooted.

2002 GZ32 was discovered automatically on April 13, 2002 by the Mauna Kea Observatory and measures more than 230.50 km in diameter. The interpretation points to pattern breaking, to the reforming of creative processes, to the perception of errors or blind spots in routines, habits, assumptions, systems or processes, no matter how firmly rooted, elaborated, indispensable, official or established they are; perception- and perspective changes and therefore changes in posture; new perspectives that undermine or render obsolete the validity and usefulness of the old ones. This can relate to more general situations and to one's own inner attitude. Mundane 2002 GZ32 can point to people in high positions who have to make thankless but necessary decisions, as well as kaleidoscopes; the kaleidoscopic. John Delaney has linked 2002 GZ32 to niche markets, modularity, opportunism, the macabre, the 11th hour and desperate negotiations.

The orbital time is 111 years and 259 days.

119315 2001 SQ73 (NAME SUGGESTION: PUMP)

Point of increasing pressure; knowing what pressure is on whom; observing pressure fluctuations and differences; being forced to verbal defense; philosophically assertive, confronting; aversion to superficial gibberish such as Twitter; catalyst of involutionary information and artistry; dealing with hypocrites.

Uranus-crossing Centaur, estimated to be about 50 km in diameter, discovered by Spacewatch on September 19, 2001 with the discovery position in 21 Aries in the 9th house. 2001 SQ73 is one of the more complex newcomers in astrology. The interpretation of 2001 SQ73 fluctuates a great deal between the negative and positive poles of this Centaur.

Characteristics: the building up of pressure and/or irritation, usually within a discussion; knowing what pressure is on whom, philosophically being a drill bit that polarizes with the conclusions drawn, throws closed systems upside down or makes them collapse, or leaves a trail of uncertainty; dealing with hypocrites and people who are cowardly avoiding a discussion; impulsiveness and restlessness, rapid alternation of activities, aversion to superficial banter such as Twitter or social media gibberish or, on the contrary, proclaiming structural lies, unsubstantiated propaganda or statements; verbally very combative; uncompromising in defense of one's own argumentation; not afraid of the discussion battleground or karmic repercussions; straightforwardly honest; postponed reactions or delayed reactions of others; restless, bubbly, self-perpetuating; mentally obsessive.

2001 SQ73 is associated by John Delaney with, among other things, tunnel construction, mining and engineering, criminal litigation and corporate negotiations, boredom, cabins and shifting the center of pressure in a space. Furthermore, there are within the chemistry context associations with oscillating frequencies and barrier breaking. 2001 SQ73 is sexually involved in pressure transfer and performance in vagina, anus or mouth/throat through the inserted penis or dildo and increases the need for penetration. 2001 SQ73 also has a relationship with peristalsis and gas displacement in the intestines. A transit over an important player such as the Sun, Moon, Ruler, etc. can make one very restless and agitated and causes the concentration to be constantly disturbed, but also creates openings and searches for grounding via root chakra/kundalini-stimulation as compensation.

2001 SQ73 has besides this more "left hemisphere" oriented package a completely different side, which is more often dominant in radix charts.

2001 SQ73 can catalyze astral or involutionary information in contrast to an aversion to, or lack of any affinity with, technology, politics, social systems and other forms of preconceived order and rules within which one should move. And so 2001 SQ73 can also stimulate philosophical insights or artistic talents that are highly original, authentic and fascinating. The Centaur can stimulate growth in the field of spiritual insight, averse to the existing spiritual consensus and clichés or lead to intense erotic experiences, when linked to one of the more sexual heavenly bodies. If 2001 SQ73 does enter technological or political waters (Gates, Obama, Merkel), it is linked to bugs or – behind the scenes – extreme and antisocial behavior, deformation and what can be summed up as negative 12th house and Black Moon qualities. If someone remains authentic and creative, 2001 SQ73 gives extra integrity. In a horoscope that does not stimulate authenticity, the Centaur can lead to the total liquidation of integrity and stimulate schizoid, extremely inconsistent expressions of behavior, with an ever-growing gap between one's own self and one's external actions. Interestingly, strong 2001 SQ73 positions can be found in the charts of Carlos Castaneda, Jean-Michel Basquiat, Austin Osman Spare; Anita Moorjani, Aleister Crowley; David Lynch; Franz von Byros, Christopher Walken, Barack Obama, Angela Merkel and Bill Gates, among others. I suggest the name *Pump* for this Centaur, because of the indeed predominant property of changing some form of pressure. The aspect of increasing and/or moving pressure is different per sign/house in 2001 SQ73. In Cancer, for example, the centaur gives physical pressure in the stomach, in Virgo in the intestines, in Aries in the head, etc.. This makes 2001 SQ73 an important player in medical astrology because the position and aspect information may allow a quick grip on part of the psychosomatics of a problem. Forensically and in mundane astrology, all pumps, pressure gauges, barometers, high-pressure and low-pressure areas and situations with an increasing pressure or threat fall under 2001 SQ73.

The orbital period is 72 years and about 220 days.

119976 2002 VR130 (NAME SUGGESTION: PLAYBOY)

La dolce vita, possibly thanks to a bestseller; intense, passionate, sexual, driven; gives a strong urge to express oneself verbally or in writing, does not allow oneself to be patronized or silenced; existentialist moments.

2002 VR130 is a Uranus, Neptune and Pluto crossing Centaur of about 24 km diameter and was discovered by Marc W. Buie on September 7, 2002. 2002 VR130 makes, if dominantly aspected, intense, passionate, sexual, driven; gives a strong urge to express oneself verbally or in writing, does not allow oneself to be patronized or silenced; increases the possibility of a career as a popular writer or actor; gives extreme emotional or sensory experiences; increased fertility. There is also a great urge for expansion for which an interpretation is sought, mostly an emotional interpretation. Sex life and orgasms are intense, relationships are not successful, connections are abruptly terminated or broken off by circumstances; at times this Centaur gives strange dreams with sometimes a link to the paranormal; the area of death; the (passing to the) other side is experienced as frightening and unpleasant. Sometimes life feels existentialistic, like something that is constantly threatened by a lurking "nothing" or "void", which should be avoided by taking action or by means of healthy hedonism. The self-preservation measures can therefore easily go over the top, which also prevents the establishment of alliances with a life partner (2002 VR130 was discovered conjunct Eris/Black Moon in Aries). One will often renounce one's own origins, the homeland, possibly one's own race or culture or the psychospheric influences of the parental home. There is a certain dissonance between a passionate active life and introvert-egocentric tendencies, as well as between a tendency to self-indulgence and a serious commitment to the Earth and the environment. A public is needed, but it is difficult to establish real contact with it, i.e. the experience of a real audience blends with the experience of digital audiences and thus the self-expression sec remains much more important than the real sharing of ideas or ideals. There is a risk of activist coquetting and a tendency to make fatalistic announcements from time to time, or to come up with a doomsday message. Many uttered ideas are utopian and remain this way as long as a strong process of self-integrity development has not yet been able to take the upper hand. Actor, writer or screenwriter are occupations that make the best match with 2002 VR130. I suggest the name Playboy for this Centaur.

The orbital period is 117 years and 99 days.

120061 2003 CO1 (NAME SUGGESTION: ASSANGE)

Nothing but the truth; Love is the Law; the positive revolution; freedom-loving; groundbreaking; visionary; progressive movements; off the grid phenomena and trends; hippy culture, 1960s ideals; politically engaged; human perspective; focused on alternative forms of housing, anti-narrow mindedness; complex technical growth- and development structures, particularly with regard to export systems, aerospace, space travel, and anti-hacking via computers and electronic systems.

2003 CO1 was discovered on February 1, 2003 by the Near Earth Asteroid Tracking program (NEAT). During its discovery, 2003 CO1 was in the 5th degree Virgo. The average diameter of 2003 CO1 is 82 km. The 5th degree of Virgo falls under the jurisdiction of the jinn Girmil (*love versus hatred, learning to see love in everything, awareness that hatred leads to disharmony only*). 2003 CO1 is in opposition to Pallas conjunct the Ursa Major-star Alula Boreale at midpoint Varda | Cyllarus. The Sun is conjunct Moon in 12/13 degrees Aquarius and conjunct Asbolus / Neptune / Aphrodite / Hidalgo / Damocles in the third house; square 2001 KF77 in Scorpio in 12 and trine 2004 EW95. In the first house, there is a striking conjunction: Ixion / Mars / Quaoar in Sagittarius.

This Centaur makes very freedom-loving, groundbreaking, visionary, exceptionally inspired and imaginative as well as progressive and tends to expose all sorts of abuses. Other features are: finding the truth, integrity, allergic to lies and PR-tricks; politically committed, idealistic; being able to detect weak spots and blind spots in one's own Zeitgeist and aspiring to major global improvements; uncovering injustice; the human perspective; courage; nomadic or aimed at alternative forms of housing; anti-narrow mindedness; whistle-blowers. Conversely, in a very negative chart, 2003 CO1 is capable to distort and manipulate the truth, if certain afflictions play a role. The Centaur can stimulate the creation of complex technical growth and developmental structures, in particular with regard to export systems, aerospace and aeronautics, computer and electronic anti-hacking. Bullying, selfishness and aggressive or blunt expressions of materialism are usually not tolerated by 2003 CO1, while continuous investments are made in communication improvement and information management.

Mundane, independent groups and the off-the-grid movement resort under 2003 CO1. Which particular feature of 2003 CO1 comes to the fore in the case of strong aspectation obviously depends on the total of factors in the horoscope. 2003 CO1 ran for decades consecutively in close conjunction with Orius, with the most exact conjunction during the heydays of the hippie-era. The hippie spirit is richly represented here, but with a dominant 2003 CO1 the almost continuous stream of ideas and insights is tested hard on the verifiability and feasibility of implementation. In order for the Centaur to achieve its full potential, the rest of the horoscopy must have sufficient realism and design power. 2003 CO1 is nevertheless a very special Centaur because it has everything to do with finding the truth and truth usually results in a wound. Truth in the Greek sense of *aletheia* as "Something which is taken out of the hidden", depends on perception, the *legein*, which means to *pick out* or to *read out*. So the point of view and instrument of the observer, by which the total dimension of truth is filtered. Workable reality thus has the ingrained tragedy that personalities, cultures, systems, as well as scientific formulas and jargons, *can only read part of the truth*, which in practice, amidst zillions of other truth filters, gives a priori conflict and violation of the total truth. To not acknowledge this failure is one of the greatest and most persistent causes of evil and suffering in the world. See how, after the video *Collateral Damage* by Wikileaks, Julian Assange was systematically demonized by an American PR-company with lies, and hypocritically betrayed by all so-called democratic and civilized Western countries, as well as companies such as Visa, PayPal and others. This in spite of international agreements signed by these countries, just because they didn't like to *complete* the "modified truth" they had created with its missing parts. Centaur 2003 CO1, although not watertight, preferably filters through the humane, human filter. The more a society dehumanizes, the more 2003 CO1 will pushe one into playing the role of poking the conscience of this society.

The orbital period is 94 years and 307 days.

136204 2003 WL7 (NAME SUGGESTION: DISRUPTOR)

Sudden explosive disruption; escalation of existing tensions; sparkling edge of unpredictability; on the edge of danger, name-calling; ordinary people threatened by life-threatening circumstances; sensitivity to the "genius" or true nature of the system and how it damages private life; sudden outbreaks of extreme violence, danger of attacks, violent revolution, total implosion of systems; irritation, anxiety, insecurity and blurred emotional perceptions; intensely creative; revolutionary or intrusive art.

2003 WL7 is a Uranus crossing Centaur, 118 km in diameter. It was discovered on November 16, 2003 by Spacewatch. John Delaney described this Centaur with the key words: disarming, interruptions, threatening, escalation, escalation of existing tensions, sparkling edge of unpredictability, at the edge of danger, cursing, ordinary people threatened by life-threatening circumstances, free radicals, threat. Given the extremely explosive, disruptive and dark aspect clusters in the 2003 WL7 discovery-horoscope, this indeed covers much of the interpretation. The discovery-position 2003 WL7 is 24°00 Aries R. in the 10th house, with Sun in the 5th in 24 Scorpio conjunct Pholus / Pandora / Tezcatlipoca / Vertex; opposition Bateman / Thais; square Asbolus; trine Yeti / Datura. Moon in 12 Leo in the 2nd house opposes Neptunus / Damocles / 2002 PN34 / Split / Scientia; trine Pallas; trine Quaoar; square Toro. Varda is conjunct Villon. Orcus conjunct BAM / Requiem and trine Rhiphonos. Black Moon trines the 8th house with Yarilo and Sundsvall on the cusp. A strong 2003 WL7 could turn someone into a stuntman/woman or thrill-seeker, or someone who registers all kinds of gross and fatal imperfections and can make it public. Yet this Centaur, with the necessary stabilizing counterweight from the horoscope in which he is positioned, can also stimulate great expressive artistry. Art is probably the best channel for this energy anyway, because in artistic expression there is at least always a constructive and creative dimension. In the worst case scenario, 2003 WL7 stands for sudden outbreaks of extreme violence, danger, attacks, violent revolution, total implosion of systems. Because there is a closed trine of Fire, consisting of a heavily afflicted Moon – Pallas – Quaoar, a political vision glows under all the revolting clenched energy, which aims at a new system. I suggest for this Centaur the name Disruptor for reasons which will be clear. A transit of 2003 WL7 to an important point or player in the birth- or progressed chart gives a period of irritation, restlessness and uncertainty as well as blurred emotional perceptions. 2003 WL7 tries in a positive way to close the gap between the human emotional reality or identity and the system identity, especially that of the political, social or scientific system. Dissonance in this area triggers both the negative and positive side of this Centaur and often to the extreme. The sensitivity to the "genius" of the system and how it violates or infiltrates private life is a very alert and intense one. The Cancer Ascendant of 2003 WL7 contains a conjunction Saturn / Elatus / Varuna, which creates the challenge of making the registration of the system/individual-dissonance earthly, realistic, honest but paradoxically also very "media-spectacular".

The orbital time is 89 years and 332 days.

145486 2005 UJ438 (NAME SUGGESTION: MOONDJINN)

Hypersensitivity; a wound in the energy body; psycho-energetic sustainability; a master in the field of energy control and psycho-energetic health; persuasion and persuasion issues; lunar energy and orgone fluctuations.

A Saturn and Uranus crossing Centaur, with a diameter of 20.80 km, discovered by Spacewatch on 28 October 2005. Complex Centaur, which gives a wound in the energy body and thus a disturbance in the interactions between the mental, astral, orgonic and physical body. 2005 UJ438 makes highly sensitive (HSP) and if crucially positioned in the birth chart, one must learn to deal with this. With a dominant 2005 UJ438, childhood or youth can be problematic because family safety or warmth or the mother bond is damaged, which gives a weakened energy field. During puberty one goes through a risky period because of this energy field being too open, making one susceptible to all kinds of undesirable energetic, psycho-energetic, astral and mental influences.

Besides the fact that the psycho-energetic problems are central here, persuasion and persuasion issues (which are closely related to *invasion* issues) also play an important role. However, one can only offer solid resistance against undesirable infringements by others if one is stable on a psycho-energetic level. The communication axis 3rd – 9th house is difficult, when this Centaur is very strong, and solid long-term work must be done to develop one's own communication abilities. With a strong affliction this Centaur increases the risk of becoming suicidal. Once purged through life experiences, training and insights, 2005 UJ438 gives the opportunity to become a master in the field of energy control and psycho-energetic health, as well as the field of communication. Especially where it concerns the translation of the effect of psychological, in-depth psychological and paranormal phenomena, processes and problems into understandable language. Here there is a lot of pioneering talent to make the invisible and elusive, as it were, concrete and a lot of talent for research. Drugs must be handled very carefully. Only at a later age, through certain (natural) psychoactive substances, can useful insights and experiences be gained. In the field of relationships, 2005 UJ438 sometimes tends to deviate from the default, with a possible tendency towards homosexuality, especially among men. The sensitivity of 2005 UJ438 is almost total and includes, besides the sensitivity to the energies of others and artificial sources such as devices with a lot of electro-smog, routers, transmission masts etc., also a sharp sensitivity to the *genius loci* ("mood, spirit" of a location).

Qi-gong and shield- or inner alchemy exercises are definitely required when this Centaur is placed strongly! Only when the psycho-energetic aspect of a person's life with such a position has become manageable, can all the positive talents of 2005 UJ438 come to fruition and this has an incredibly positive effect on one's life and the forces in the horoscope, which until then, due to the disruptive effect of the injury that the Centaur gives, remained latent and inert. 2005 UJ438 also has a link with Moon energy and orgone fluctuations.

I suggest the name Moondjinn for 2005 UJ438, based on the very Moon-related 10th degree Taurus, where 2005 UJ438 was positioned during its discovery. Concario is the name of the jinn or geni that rules over this degree and it is explicitly connected with Moon magic and all fluctuations that are connected with the Moon and therefore also with emotions, moods, mood sensitivity and sensitivity in general.

The orbital period is 73 years and 146 days.

148975 2001 XA255

Tendency to condemn, prosecute; acceptance-rejection issues; communication problems and/or challenges; philosophical or spiritual genius who has to deal with the curse of superficial communication and perception and is frustrated by this; an exporter who experiences transport problems in the last phase of the transport process; great research talent; securing property; marriage problems because a third person interfering in the relationship; an unusual childhood and youth or strange domestic circumstances; duty versus enjoyment; security systems.

2001 XA255 was discovered by D.C. Jewitt, S.S. Sheppard and J. Kleyna on December 9, 2001 and measures 37.70 km in diameter. 2001 XA255 was in the 16th degree Cancer in the 9th house conjunct the star Canopus and the Plutino 2003 AZ84 / Jupiter / Varuna; opposition Sethos / Chrisodom. The perihelion of 2001 XA255 is just inside the orbit of Saturn, while the aphelion with 48,384 EA almost reaches the outer boundary of the Kuiper belt, thus shaping the orbit of 2001 XA255 into an extreme ellipse. Characteristics: philosophical or spiritual genius who has to deal with the curse of superficial communication and perception and is frustrated by this; a scientific researcher who encounters the same kind of communication problems; a lawyer who gets bogged down in the communicative bargaining of his organization or the other party; an exporter who constantly has transport problems on the final trajectories; a politician going down the drain because of a homosexuality scandal; wanting to find out; prosecute, tends to condemn; undergoes rejections because one's own complex and holistic scope does not fit in; strong mind-power; killing the communication because of launching such overpowering and penetrating remarks that the other person experiences this as a kind of verbal rape and retreats; popularity through courage; ruthless honesty or gross humor in personal contact; marriage problems because a third person interferes in the relationship; an intermittent tendency to isolation, einzelgänger behaviour and a somber fatalistic realism; a personality that fluctuates between stable and constructive and (system) disruptive, attacking the system; a high degree of skepticism where it concerns new results from technological inventions, engineering and futurological performances, including a love/hate relationship with science fiction; the design and unfolding of constructions that provide financial security and continuity; unusual domestic circumstances; an unusual childhood and youth.

With a strong 2001 XA255 it is essential that personal will and actions get fully in line with the personal dream, and that one arranges life in such a way that this "fusion and synergy between Mars and Neptune energies" is given as much space as possible. One of the obstacles that someone with a dominant 2001 XA255 has to overcome, however, is first and foremost an extreme tendency to defend and achieve rights and ethics, which comes with a lot of associated condemnations and frustrations about the scope of the large mass, media, politics or the academically entrenched cohort of colleagues, which is perceived as narrow. This just consumes energy. Secondly, one can make life much easier for oneself by learning to dose in terms of communication, thus stopping an extreme thoroughness and an overload of context and background information where this isn't useful anyway and adapting ones way of communicating to the target group/other. Most practical problems are on the communication axis Sagittarius/9th house – Gemini/3rd house. It is very important to acquire a sense of humor, as this is often helpful when trying to convert abstract complex information into a recognizable everyday context and understandable sentences. Information will thus have to be distributed and built up in phases, whereby the other or the audience can gradually join the often brilliant new insights which the positive 2001 XA255 in a sophisticated horoscope has to offer. 2001 XA255 must therefore learn to cultivate patience, while patience is not the strongest characteristic of this Centaur. 2001 XA255 is linked to an *extremely secure environment* (on transneptunian-astrology.blogspot.nl). I think this is indeed an option, but only when linked to property protection. This has to do with the strong 2nd house occupation, which, with Ixion / Venus / Quaoar on the cusp in Sagittarius, links proprietary technological expansion of growth and development systems coupled with foresight. Saturn makes a hard opposition in 8 with Venus and with Sun / Pluto/ Mercury and Chiron in 2 and the dismal heavyweight Asbolus at the end of the 2nd house heightens this option. Saturn-Venus-oppositions revolve around a "*duty versus enjoy-conflict*" and often burden someone with exaggerated accountability. The extreme securing of one's possessions is in that case a very obvious expression.

Mark Andrew Holmes links 2001 XA255 to persecution, judgmental attitude, repudiation, rejection and condemnation. Afflicting transits of the Centaur underline these associations, especially when aspecting the Sun or chart ruler. However, they also incite a breaking point, in which one does everything to escape circumstances one experiences as an imprisonment or overshadowing of some kind. What is needed is an inner homeostasis reset under the umbrella of *energy flows where attention goes.* 2001 XA255 is one of the more difficult objects of the Centaur-class.

The orbital period is 156 years and 161 days.

241097 2007 DU112

Converging what works in synergy to grand results; one's own unique destination which climaxes in a completion or peak performance; the linking of a (often brilliant) performance, completion or victory to the right person at the right time, or "in the right time, in the right place"; the budding of someone's "flower" after many years of preparation.

2007 DU112 is a Centaur of about 27 km in diameter. The object was discovered by Spacewatch on February 23, 2007. This is a special Centaur because once activated via a long transit or a shift in the progressed horoscope (provided that someone has the proper mental equipment) 2007 DU112 can activate an unstoppable converging of forces, visions and talents in which karma, years of study or effort or research move to towards an inner apotheosis, (big substantial eureka-moment) a great performance or end-result. A situation in which someone seems to appear out of nowhere and suddenly takes the lead with his or her work over the state of affairs within a discipline, process or enterprise. 2007 DU112 thus links an (often brilliant) performance, completion or victory to the right time and the right place in relation to one's actual career. There is a strong link between this Centaur and what has always been a subcutaneous current connected to personal fate, or ones true destination. 2007 DU112 works best in conjunction or trine with the MC because this catalyzes and concretes the energy of 2007 DU112 at its best.

However, the way in which someone climaxes does not necessarily have to be in line with his work or career, but can simply be the sum of a collection of parts (read: activities linked to affinities and talents or home-made skills) that someone suddenly brings to the fore. 2007 DU112 is especially interesting to use in the progressed, transit and solar return charts.

The orbital time is 258 years and 219 days.

250112 2002 KY14

Wanting to switch off something or someone; learning to deal with an unstable course or a chronically uncertain situation; variability; arbitrariness, intellectual registration; working with electrons; power failure, malfunctions, a device that suddenly stops; assassins; daredevils.

2002 KY14 was discovered by Chadwick A. Trujillo and Michael E. Brown on May 19, 2002 and measures 38.90 km in diameter. The interpretation in the birth chart revolves around: someone who wants to disable something; learning to deal with an unstable course or a chronically uncertain situation; variability; arbitrariness or apparent arbitrariness coordinated from intuition, which turns out to be correct afterwards; intellectual registration; working with electrons; overcoming psychological predispositions and or harmful ethical psychological assumptions that are mainstream; psycho-ethical complexities, insights and discussions (e.g., 'Should someone have eliminated Hitler for humanitarian reasons if it was already known and certain what he would do?); metaphysics. In transits: the critical moment of decision; a situation where the course suddenly changes or has to be changed; something which has to be switched off or a person who somehow gets "switched off" (e.g. an athlete who gets injured in a tournament). Forensic: loss or shutdown of something or someone; power failure, malfunctions, a device that suddenly stops; assassins or hit men; snipers; combat defense techniques such as Krav Maga (Hebrew), Systema (Russian) etc.; dare devils, paratroopers, extreme surfing, slalom skiers; snowboarders; ski jumpers; people who make important decisions at critical moments, people who decide.

The orbital time is 43 years and 110 days.

389820 2011 WU92 (NAME SUGGESTION: MEPHISTO)

Persuasion issues; wanting to persuade someone or a group to do something, for good or evil or a reluctance to ask others to do something; a conflict between self-motivation and self-sabotage; "must do" as a stress factor.

2011 WU92 was discovered by the Mt. Lemmon Survey on October 12, 2010 and has a diameter of 11 km or more. The remarkable thing is that the Centaur was rediscovered in 2011 and 2013. The latter earned him the designation 2013 AJ13, but this is the same Centaur as 2011 WU92. 2011 WU92 crosses the orbit of Saturn and almost tips the orbit of Jupiter (perihelion is at 5.6 AU and aphelion at 12.5 AU). 2011 WU92 has to do with persuading someone or a group to do something, for good or bad, and with a conflict between self-motivation and self-sabotage. In essence, 2011 WU92 is about the persuasion itself and whatever plays a role in this process. In affliction with a protagonist such as the Sun or ruler, there is a reluctance to ask others to do something. But on the other hand, it is in fact impossible for others to try and make this person do something if the usefulness of the request is not understood or if there is – for whatever reason – a resistance to it This can easily get out of hand, due to a matter of principle, for instance. There is an intense resistance that can completely drain the other person during his or her attempt to persuade someone with a strongly aspected 2011 WU92.

Apart from the impulsive level as described above, 2011 WU92 is the critical note when acting in relation to others, but also in self-sabotage. In every action involving several people, there is the question of give-and-take. In the house in which 2011 WU92 is located in the birth chart, the notion of "must" can be a constant stress factor, so this must be transcended with finding a passionate way of dealing with the assignment of the house. I suggest the name Mephisto because he is the archetype of persuasion.

The orbital period of 2011 WU92 is 26 years and 36 days.

472651 2015 DB216

Failing political iconoclasm; wolves in sheep's clothing; a doomsday prophecy out of sincere concern; literary or musical talent, or talented movie directors.

2015 DB216 was discovered by the Mount Lemmon Survey on February 27, 2015. 2015 DB216 was at the moment of discovery in 6°43 Virgo conjunct Orcus in the 9th house with Pallas / Ixion / Pholus on the Ascendant and the discovery-Sun conjunct Neptune in Pisces in the 3rd house and the Northern nodes on the MC in Libra. The diameter is not clear yet (date Oct.6, 2019) and estimated somewhere between 44 to 140 km. Characteristics: a very strictly worked out philosophy, that is either deployed from a mix of altruism and ingenious foresight or strategically and politically aimed within some form of iconoclasm, that is doomed to fail; an irresistible urge to attack the prevailing mode of reality and cause an earthquake; learning to understand that personal aspirations can only be expressed through literary or artistic means and that the political way means ruin or suicide; razor-sharp, very powerful and penetrating analyses or statements which only upsets the listeners or render them silent or – in the best case scenario, they pick them up and share them later; very radically and thoroughly in the underpinning of philosophical rejection of established assumptions, default beliefs, official truths and a faulty mode of reality; a merciless disapproval of the Kafkaesque in politics and society; cultural philosophy and criticism; explosive revolutionary; unpredictable, eruptive; wild and indomitable; emotional truth versus a system development growing within a rigid conception; sexually engaged; concretizing; purposeful; intuitive incursions at just the right moment. Tact, cooperation and diplomacy must be cultivated by 2015 DB216 and negative Virgo and Leo qualities must be purged. Forensically, the Centaur has in particular a link with disruptions of the status quo and politics in London/Great Britain.

The orbital period is 84 years and 20 days.

999004 2000 CO104 (NAME SUGGESTION: SATYROS)

Discharge, ecstasy, orgasm; relaxation or discharge by ecstasy; seeking sensation, things that give kicks; zero point consciousness; magic point, directionism, chaos magic; in strong transits a temporary craving for ecstasy inducing psychotropics; creative, colorful, fond of variety; the unusual, rebellious.

2000 CO104 was discovered by a team from the Kitt Peak Observatory on February 6, 2000 and the average diameter is estimated at about 44-48 km. It is a very sexual, creative, exciting and ecstatic Centaur who moves between the orbits of Uranus and Neptune but does not cross them. Astrologically, 2000 CO104 stands primarily for relaxation or discharge by ecstasy, for the ecstasy and for the orgasm. The way one gets or experiences an orgasm is intensely influenced by 2000 CO104 and sign, house and aspects give extra information about a person's orgasms and specifics that may trigger/stimulate or hinder it. With strong transits there can also be a craving for ecstacy inducing psychotropics, such as psilocybin, LSD, hashish/marihuana, XTC, etc... In Fire signs 2000 CO104 is mainly linked to orgasms or ecstasy as discharge of accumulated yang-qi. In Water signs the emotional aspects of sex and also the intense and mystical factor are very important. In Air signs the imagination and fantasy are crucial and in Earth signs the physical state and its appearance are primary, but also the cycles (like menstruation-ovulation, biorhythms etc.), the deep intense sexual experience, or redemption from the routine. In Taurus and Capricorn there is also a strong hedonistic component and longing for the very deep orgasm. Mark Andrew Holmes links 2000 CO104 to intense emotions, passionate creativity, capacity to inspire, to uplift, to stimulate, art, histrionics, dramatics, to control and manipulate, sexuality, orgasmic pleasure, dedication, thrill-seeking, sensitivity, vibrancy, vividness, colorfulness, ecstasy, enthusiasm. Aspect with Sun (also transits of Sun over the Centaur) give pleasant and intense orgasms, while Uranus over Satyros shortens and accelerates the orgasm, possibly because these two forces together are too electrically charged. Then there is a strong link between 2000 CO104 and chaos magic or the magic act in general. 2000 CO104 links the orgasm to a zero point in the time / space / consciousness / energy-continuum, the point that is used contemplatively during a magical command. The energy or meaning of an object or planet which during a transit makes a conjunction with 2000 CO104 can get a magical effect during that transit and start "a new course of life" in someone's existence. Simultaneous aspecting of 2000 CO104 by the Apollo-asteroid Talos emphasizes this quality of the Centaur extra strongly. During its discovery in the 27th degree Leo in the 10th house the Centaur was conjunct with the star Alphard (*passion, lust, voluptuousness, friskiness, debauchery, letting go of moral blockages*); conjunct Hunfeld (*increased multi-sensory imagination, mood registration and empathy; psychometry*) and opposition 2000 OO67 (*to transcend something*). The discovery-chart also shows the Ascendant in the 14th degree Scorpio conjunct Bennu (*rebirth*). The discovery-Sun is (at 1 minute) exactly conjunct Uranus at 16°29 Aquarius conjunct Amun (*wanting to reach the top by crossing boundaries*). Lust in the discovery-chart is on midpoint Randi (*horniness*)|Chrisodom (*anal sex*); Eros (*passion, sex*) positioned very strongly conjunct Galahad (*letting go of all obsession*) while the sexual asteroid Yarilo (*sex*) is conjunct with Zero (*zero point*). Bacchus (*sex & fluids*) is conjunct Messalina (*sexually insatiable*) and Thisbe (*suicide – the French call orgasm 'le petit mort'*). Venus is conjunct Charybdis (*being swallowed up by the urge to connect or love*) and trine Sedna (*where the concrete world is abandoned*) and finally Neptune makes a conjunction with Tara (*mystic, loving, colorful*). Via Mars/1999 TC36 and Moon trine Deucalion 2000 CO104 has a metaphysical, magical and occult undertone, underlined by Flammario square Neptune. Richard Wagner had 2000 CO104 conjunct MC / Paranal; square Somnium; halfsextile Flammario; inconjunct Panacea / 1998 WW24 / 1996 SZ4; inconjunct Echeclus / Borasisi / Klythia. (See also Neptune Trojan 2010 EN65). Leopold Sacher-Masoch had 2000 CO104 conjunct BAM in the pronounced sexual 17th degree Pisces; trine Sanguin / Cusp 3rd house in Taurus; square Industria in Sagittarius; trine Orcus in Scorpio; inconjunct Requiem / 2001 UO18 / Colocolo in Libra; opposition 1992 QB1; trine Charybdis / cusp 6th house; square 1999 XX143 (*provocation, self-expression*) in Gemini, with Lovejoy at the Aries point. Forensic 2000 CO104 rules all bodily fluids that are discharged out of lust, like sperm, pre-cum, squirt and other vaginal excretions; the ecstatic in general; the zero point.

The orbital period is 119 years and 36 days.

1559

SCATTERED DISC OBJECTS (SDOs) & DETACHED OBJECTS

471143 DZIEWANNA

Life/death issues (also on an emotional level); fatalistic tensions; emotional cold showers; being condemned or harshly judged; the dictatorship of the conservative majority; social deformations; wounded or repressed female identity expressing itself; deformed or misplaced due to circumstances; feeling intrinsically cursed; fighting against people with no contextual or connotative intelligence; extreme or "herculean" power struggle at all costs; being forced to produce something outstanding or original in order to survive, which turns out to be unsatisfying after all; suicidal thoughts; cancer caused by the suffocating harshness of others or untouchable systems; destroying something delicate and good; highest degree of difficulty; chthonic forces, agricultural rituals and traditions, witchcraft (good or bad); winter turning into spring or spring turning into winter; misuse of sex to channel emotional wounds; sexual contact with the earth; spring and nature; not getting noticed or understood; hypersensitivity as a curse with erotic or sexual expression as a cure or relief; painstakingly taking ones responsibility.

Dziewanna (provisional designation 2010 EK139), was discovered on March 13, 2010 by Andrzej Udalski, Scott Sheppard, Marcin Kubiak and Chad Trujillo at the Las Campañas Observatory in Chile. The discovery was made during the Polish OGLE project of Warsaw University. Based on its absolute magnitude and assumed albedo, it is very likely a dwarf planet with a calculated diameter of approximately 470 kilometers. The Minor Planet Center classifies Dziewanna as an SDO/Extended Centaur, while Marc Buie of Deep Ecliptic Survey suggests a 2:7-Neptune resonant, based on a 10 million year computer-simulation of Dziewannas orbit.

The object was named after Devana or Dziewanna, supposedly a Slavic goddess of the wilderness, forests and the hunt. However, mythologically Dziewanna is a controversial subject. The common theory describes her as the Slavic equivalent of the Roman goddess Diana, and Greek Artemis, mentioned by 15th century Polish historian Jan Długosz in *Annales seu cronici incliti regni Poloniae* (History of Poland). Her name, though similar to Diana's, is apparently derived from a Slavic word that means 'virgin' or 'maiden' (dziewa, dziewica) or else from the Proto-Indo-European root dewas ("god, wonder"). Yet, most contemporary scholars don't regard *Annales seu cronici incliti regni Poloniae* as a reliable source on Slavic mythology and have doubts about the existence of such a deity in the Slavic pantheon. However Sir James George Frazer tells us that an effigy is carried in from the woods, "*which goes by the name of Summer, May, or the Bride: in the Polish districts it is called Dziewanna, the goddess of spring.*" More educational is Wilhelm Mannhardt (Frasier borrowed at lot from this German author), who is skeptical to about Dziewanna being the equivalent of Diana/Artemis, likely because of confusing ritual puppets of straw representing fertility daemons, or their related seasons, with goddesses in the context of the Christian persecution of pagan beliefs and their symbols, icons and rituals. Within this context, in Podlachien (north-east Poland, bordering Russia) *Totensonntag* had been introduced. This "Sunday of the Dead", also called *Ewigkeitssonntag* (Eternity Sunday) or *Totenfest*, is a Northern German and Dutch Protestant religious holiday commemorating the dead. It falls on the last Sunday before the First of the Sundays of Advent (i.e. always on or between Nov. 20 and Nov. 26), and it is the last Sunday of the liturgical year in the German Evangelical Church and the Protestant Church in The Netherlands. Where it is marked, such as in Berlin, it replaces All Souls' Day (Nov. 2). A straw puppet of Marena (Mamurienda, Muriena) was carried to a pool or swamp and ritually "drowned". The first Christian Polish ruler Mieszko c. 930 – 25 May 992) who ruled Poland from about 960 until his death, had ordered an alternative Death Day on March 7 each year for the destruction of pagan images, ritual puppets and statues. Dziewanna and Marzanna are mentioned in a similar context: *Quae quidam...idolurum confractio et immersio tune facta apud nonnulas Polonorum villas simulacra Dziewannae et Marzannae in longo ligno extollentibus et in paludes in Dominica Quadragesimae Laetare projicientibus et demergentibus repraesentur (et) renovatur in hunc diem.*

It is possible that Dziewanna and Marzanna could have been two faces of one goddess, the lady of life and death at the same time; similar analogies in other Indo-European beliefs (such as Kora-Persefona or two faces of Hell) may indicate this, but the lack of source data makes it impossible to draw conclusions. To make the confusion complete: another name of Devana is *Ciza*, whose etymology is traced to the Slavic root *cic* or *cec*, meaning the mother's breast. Under the name variations Dzydzilelya, Zizilia or Didilia, she is known as the goddess of love and wedding, fertility and infancy among West Slavs; this name is explained as meaning "she who pampers babies" (cf. dziecilela), and with these functions she is compared to the Roman Venus or Lucina. Devana has been regarded as a manifestation of the great goddess Rodiva–Deva, especially in her terrestrial fertile aspect, and as such compared to the Germanic Nerthus.

Dziewanna is a very tough and difficult force to handle. In a positive sense one can gain a profound understanding of the chthonian reality, witchcraft, male-female-metaphysics, the sexual charges in nature, i.e. something the Andalusians call *duende*. Because a strongly placed Dziewanna gifs a tendency to melancholy, it is very important to cultivate the "Why so serious?" and the atman-connection as the anchor of the self and personality, especially because this object is strongly Taurean (with Sun in the discovery-chart conjunct Sedna and the fixed star Zaurak) and therefore easily prone to aggression from anyone or any force or trend that experiences holism in thought and feeling as a threat to the functioning of their own short-cut mind frame. Yet the bulk of Dziewannas' influence centers around: life/death issues (also on the emotional level), fate, fatalistic tensions; an existential state of suffering, that has to be accepted in a Luciferian way (*I need to fight death to conquer life*); emotional cold showers; confrontations; being condemned or harshly judged; the dictatorship of the conservative majority, social deformations; wounded or repressed female identity expressing itself in a deformed or misplaced way due to circumstances; feeling intrinsically cursed, fighting against people with no contextual or connotative intelligence; extreme or "herculean" infighting at all costs; being forced to produce something outstanding or original by way of survival, which turns out to be unsatisfying after all; suicidal thoughts, feeling crushed; cancer caused by the suffocating harshness of others or untouchable systems, cancer returning after healing; destroying something delicate and good; highest degree of difficulty; not getting noticed or understood; destruction of something which took decades to build or harvesting nothing but sadness when one should feel proud, satisfied or victorious after much painstaking work and sacrifice; getting pissed on by the crowd for doing good; the constant threat of getting isolated as a chronic source of stress; chthonic forces, agricultural rituals and traditions, witchcraft (good or bad); winter turning into spring or spring turning into winter; misuse of sex to channel emotional wounds, sexual contact with earth, spring and nature; hypersensitivity as a curse with erotic or sexual expression as a cure or relief; painfully taking ones responsibility; the awareness that power isolates, makes cold and thus is the universal human booby trap and in a paradox the cure for not getting harassed by others; (sexual) skeletons in the closet.

Due to its extreme discovery-chart, with players like Sun trine Typhon / Logos, Sun conjunct Sedna / Sethos opposition Echeclus, Damocles square Sun, Taurean depth-psychology, an overheated Venus (conjunct the explicit sexual asteroid 1998 XB), and an overcharged ambition (nodes opposite Black Sun on the Diamond, discovery-position Dziewanna opposition Sun, Mars in

Leo on Balbastre), Dziewanna is one of the most, perhaps *the* most difficult object among the newcomers in astrology to deal with. Almost every vibe this SDO emanates seems cursed in some way. The House Dziewanna occupies in the birth-chart is often a pain spot. In Polish forensic astrology Dziewanna could point at Dziewanna drobnokwiatowa (Verbascum thapsus L.), a yellow flower associated with the goddess, or (chronic) physical complaints that are directly related to the zodiacal degree Dziewanna is in, and the body part or organ ruled by that degree in relation to pain, frustration or sorrow of the "Dziewanna-kind" as described above.

The orbital period is about 592 years and 8 months.

136199 ERIS

Work power; self-preservation; perseverance to the end, never giving up; power instinct and power manipulations; political fighters and pushers; a schizoid separation of one's ambition & the self by identifying with a tunnel vision and/or a network of lies, ending in character suicide, the fallen idol; falling down; a chronically smoldering paranoid sensitivity to every conceivable form of resistance; flight-fight reactions when psycho-synthesis issues are emerging which enforce self reflection; anti-social.

Eris was discovered on January 5, 2005 by Michael Brown, Chad Trujillo and David Rabinowitz. Immediately after Pluto, Eris is the largest dwarf planet, with an equatorial diameter of 2326 km and an eccentric orbit with an inclination of 44°. The perihelion is 37.77 AU and the aphelion 97.56 AU. Eris has a moon of about 100 km in diameter, called Dysnomia, named after the Greek goddess of discord. Barack Obama, who after receiving his Nobel Peace Prize bombed seven countries in service of Big Industry, brutally increased the number of drone murders sixfold and reanimated the nuclear arms race, has Eris conjunct Chaos / Hilda square Orcus. The birth charts of Hillary Clinton, George W. Bush and Joris Demmink (Dutch politician accused of witnessing a sexually tinged murder on a 9 year old boy, and other pedophile crimes) have a conjunction Eris / Typhon and they all seem to have nourished themselves with the worst venom out of Eris' alter ego's jug. However, I know a very nice woman who also has Eris conjunct Typhon and is actually only interested in social, spiritual and astrological matters. As with any "suspicious" dwarf planet, Plutino, Centaur, or a more simple asteroid, a very complex interplay of horoscopic positions and relationships, in association with the indirect "second and third hand" astrological influences such as genes, educators and (sub)cultural pressures, determine what exactly comes into manifestation in one's life and how, via what forms of expression. The positive Eris is simply a source of power that mostly resembles a Mars / Pluto conjunction in Taurus, placed in an active house (*manifestation-power, hold on, never give up and get it done!*). Leaning on administratively enforced card houses of hard lies and disinformation networks, as we often see in the daily routines of politicians with a strong Eris, is however not a Taurus thing at all. The negative Eris has a chronically smoldering paranoid sensitivity to every conceivable form of resistance and thus usually ends up in a downright obsessive form of negative symbiosis. Even when "neutrally" positioned in the birth chart, Eris is always ready for battle and manifests a continuous aversion to a state of relaxation and the quiet enjoyment of life. In a mundane setting Eris is one of the most important players in disasters, turbulent times and struggles, especially those of people who position themselves against the government or system or vice versa. The conjunctions and oppositions with Eris involving Uranus, Typhon and/or Black Moon are among the most disastrous aspects of mundane astrology. In 2016 Europe witnessed several peaks of violence and riots during an opposition Eris / Uranus – Typhon / Black Moon.

Eris is characterized by the following set of terms: struggle to the extreme, never give up or let go; a struggle that is self-destructive but continued; neglecting sane or proper judgment, and fueled by some bizarre instinctive drive; persevering to the end; fighting for something until it is achieved; a "personal" struggle or "mission" or vocation, which is not always consciously carried out or fulfilled, but which is simply a perpetuating thing one puts ones energy in; aggressive missionary complex, carried out with great zeal, in which one camouflages a subcutaneous anger with a populist image and the use of power-language; strength, ausdauer, Pluto-Mars-like drive; the lust for power, power manipulation, media manipulation, the manipulative use of people or followers solely for one's own benefit, usually politically inclined, career; a compelling drive to reach the top; the inner knowing that one is alone, even if one has followers; a destructive and evil urge to pull everyone along in one's own downfall or power psychosis; ruthlessness; a large gap concerning one's own love life, affection, and being allowed to lose oneself in something that opposes and breaks through the self-raised delusional routine of an "obligation or struggle"; being separated from one's parents, loss of innocence, entrance to adult life (Zane Stein); mobilization, the mobilization urge, restless energy; extreme devotion to an ideology, personality inflation through megalomania or through the apparent sacrificing of one's individuality, private life, self-integrity and personal needs, just to be able to measure up with – and conform to – the system or the status quo, in order to exert influence; political

DI
INDIA
HOLLANDS
HEYLL en RAMPEN.

crime, state crimes, government crimes, working with official standpoints to camouflage a super lie; submission to "the course of history"; all possible forms of conformism to the prevailing social consensus; pathological malignancy; simmering chronic frustration and anger; organizing persecutions on the basis of religious or philosophical ideas (Hillary Clinton – during her last election time sponsored by 93% of the war industry worldwide – openly said they should kill Julian Assange with a drone, and laughed manically at the murder of Gadaffi.); obstruction of political opponents or movements and the development of content; developed minds; the most rancid forms of power, influence, sponsors etc. By contrast, however: *A sharp awareness of all that belongs to the dark side of Eris, while not partaking in it, but critisizing it.* The latter is usually the case with positive Eris aspects, flanked by more positive indicators in the chart.

The fact that in the discovery-horoscope Eris is in Aries, conjunct with both the Plutino 1993 SB (*extreme screening*) and 2005 UJ438 (*hypersensitive*) sextile Machiavelli / Asbolus, square Nessus, trine Typhon in Leo, trine Arawn (1994 JR1) in Sagittarius, and in the opposite sign of the discovery-Sun, explains a lot. The North nodes in Taurus conjunct Colocolo (*never gives up the struggle even when being in the minority, never surrenders or gives in*) underline the most characteristic feature of this SDO. Within the psychosphere of Eris, Taurus' energy is purged because of the Black Moon in Taurus, conjunct with the Plutino 1998 US43 (*schizoid conflict between image and identity*).

The orbital period is 557 years and 146 days.

225088 GONGGONG – (SNOW WHITE)

Group awareness and group interaction.

Gonggong is a candidate dwarf planet, known also by its provisional designation 2007 OR10 (the unofficial name used by astrologers was *Snow White*). The object was discovered on July 17, 2007 by M.E. Schwamb, Michael Brown and David Rabinowitz. The average diameter is estimated at 1280 to 1535 km. Gonggong is a Chinese water god who is depicted in Chinese mythology and folktales as having red hair and a human head with the body of a serpent, or a human head and torso with the tail of a serpent (or dragon). He is destructive and is blamed for various cosmic catastrophes, especially floods. In all accounts, Gonggong ends up being killed or sent into exile, usually after losing a struggle with another major deity such as the fire god Zhurong.

Unlike Eris, who rules over individual perseverance and personal struggle to the extreme, regardless of circumstances or sane social feedback from the outside world, Gonggong is all about the group you are part of, or the group you are dealing with and your individual interaction with it. Eris is a despotic pusher. Gonggong is initially a social being. Gonggong is about the group in the broadest sense of the word. The position in the birth chart says a lot about how one feels about the concept of group, which is determined by sign, house, degree and aspects. If Gonggong makes a strong contact with Sun, Moon, Ascendant, MC, IC, DC, Ruler, North node or Black Moon, the group will occupy a rather dominant position in one's life. This makes Gonggong an important player in the personal horoscope, as well as in forensic astrology and of course political astrology. The harmonious placement and aspects of Gonggong indicate talent to work with groups or to move within groups. With hard and disharmonious aspects, the group is a source of problems. Furthermore, the disharmonious Gonggong can lead to problems regarding a healthy balance between one's (core)self and individuality (individuation process), like getting absorbed in group hysteria or stupid trend following.

The orbital time is 547 years and 186 days.

229762 G!KÚN||'HÒMDÍMÀ (GKUNHOMDIMA)

Holistic insight and the capability of making communicable the flaws, dead ends and structural errors in very large cultural or social-economic and/or ecological systems, though this takes a long preparation time; Zeitgeist-sensitive and alert; revolutionary insight which takes the emotional dimension as serious as the politicized automatic pilot reality; a forceful, almost prophetic trans-personal subcutaneous drive, partially rooted in "evil past life karma", partially in something divine, to prevent a huge disaster; deep worldly and human understanding; messiah or Joan of Arc-complexes; distorted sexual expression.

229762 G!kún||'hòmdímà, provisional designation 2007 UK126, was discovered on October 19, 2007 by the American astronomers Megan Schwamb, Michael Brown, and David Rabinowitz at the Palomar Observatory in California. This non spherical object measures between 599-638 kilometers in diameter, and is a representative (just like the Cubewanos Varda and Salacia) of mid-sized objects under approximately 1000 km in diameter or a little less, that do not appear to have collapsed into fully solid bodies. Its 100 kilometer moon G!ò'é !Hú was discovered by Keith Noll, Will Grundy and colleagues with the Hubble Space Telescope in 2008.

The name G!kún||'hòmdímà is from the Ju|'hoansi (!Kung) people of Namibia. G!kún||'hòmdímà is the Beautiful Aardvark Girl of Ju|'hoan mythology, who sometimes appears in the stories of other San peoples as a python girl or elephant girl; she defends her people and punishes wrongdoers using g||ámíg||àmì spines, a rain-cloud full of hail, and her magical oryx horn. The name "G!kún||'hòmdímà" derives from g!kún 'aardvark', ||'hòm mà 'young woman' and the feminine suffix dí. The moon G!ò'é !Hú is named after her horn: it simply means 'oryx' (g!ò'é) 'horn' (!hú).

Significance in the chart: holistic insight and capable of making communicable the flaws, dead ends and structural errors in very large cultural or social-economic and/or ecological systems, though this takes a long preparation time; Zeitgeist-sensitive and alert; occupied with moving mass madness (like masses indoctrinated by warmongers, media, opinion leaders of the financial world, etc.) away from total destruction; revolutionary insight which takes the emotional dimension as serious as the politicized automatic pilot reality; the other perspective next to the mass culture's blind spot; a forceful, almost prophetic trans-personal subcutaneous drive, rooted partially in "evil past life karma", partially in something divine to prevent a huge disaster; deep worldly and human understanding; charisma emerging at a certain period in life for good or bad; in negative horoscopes messiah or Joan of Arc-complexes; forging a brilliant vision before its time and thus destroying something which could have made a major difference in the future; provocation as a fatal mistake; difficult love life; fear of binding concealment; disproportionate self sacrifice; seeking relief of built up mental and emotional frustrations via a quick working towards orgasm; a tendency towards perversion or extreme sexual activity, rooted in the feeling of being repressed by an impersonal source.

Independent research journalism and documentary making (or the combination of both) should be the best means of expressing the fruit one can harvest from this object, when strongly placed in the birth chart. In forensic astrology G!kún||'hòmdímà can denote: a disaster avoided at the last minute, or trusting the false messiah, *Hansje Brinker*, the one who ignores the order, to push the red button.

The discovery chart shows G!kún||'hòmdímà in 25°44' Taurus moving retrograde, conjunct and midpoint both 1996 TL66 25° 34' Rx Taurus and 1996 TP66 25°52' Rx Taurus / Townsend / Yamamoto, inconjunct discovery-Sun in the 26th degree Libra conjunct 2002 GZ32 (*breaking through rusty patterns, revealing blind spots and system flaws*) / 1988XB (*sex*) / Refugium (*shelter*). Mars is conjunct 2002 XU93 (*sharp penetrating revealing of all illusion*) trine 2005PQ21 / Augias (*perverse sex*). Pluto, Arawn, Toro and Machiavelli are conjunct the Galactic Center (26°57' Sagittarius). This makes the discovery position of G!kún||'hòmdímà the point of a Yod-figure created by Sun and its conjunctions and Pluto and its conjunctions, creating an epicenter of imperative transforming forces, centered around deep holistic Zeitgeist and/or system (politicized and modified reality) awareness and a very strong urge to reveal wrongdoings, misconceptions and blind spots. On midpoint 1996 TL66 25°34' Taurus (*boiling before the eruption*) and 1996 TP66 25°52' Rx Taurus (*exposing the lies, masks illusions*) / Townsend (*extreme loneliness, depression, isolation*) / Yamamoto (*exposing truth, research journalism*), G!kún||'hòmdímà moves away, backwards, retrograde from fixed star Algol (*total destruction, massacre – in this context*). As Algol in a positive sense is the Head of the Gorgon, the mirror that reflects everything in society and human live that is wrongly denied, not faced, cowardly avoided, so can the negative G!kún||'hòmdímà fail completely to live up to its wonderful almost saint-like mission. The fruit of this unique SDO will therefore always be the fruit of a test in bravery. This object truly opens the possibility of becoming a hero in the proper sense of the term.

The orbital period of G!kún||'hòmdímà is 620 years and 170 days.

90377 SEDNA

Refusal of the artificial super-hologram; lifting consciousness out of the matrix; beyond all isms; effectuating a reality modification or seeing through it; out-of-world; suffering or exile by not being able to conform to the consensus or imposed will of another; loss of limbs, hands or feet; limbs with birth defects or deformities; Softenon-victims; becoming "socially invisible", like during a Moon transit through the 12th house; isolation; financial setbacks.

Sedna (2012VP13) is a Detached Object of the Sednoid class. Sedna was discovered by Michael Brown, Chad Trujillo and David Rabinowitz on November 14, 2003, as a reddish object and measures 995 to 1060 km in diameter. The aphelion of Sedna is located at 937 AU from the Sun (31 times the distance of Neptune to the Sun). Sedna's Centaur-like extreme elliptical orbit encircles our very old planetary Solar System and does not cross any orbit of the far away planets Neptune or Pluto. Sedna was named after the dreaded Sea Goddess of the Inuit. She is sometimes represented as half woman, half fish, with the tail of a white dolphin. Sedna's myth is as extreme as her orbit.

There are several myths about her, but the common thread is that of a woman who refuses to marry the man her father had chosen for her. Her father then throws her into the sea, and when she wants to climb aboard again, he first cuts her fingers off and then her hands, after which she sinks into the depths and becomes the ruler of all the sea creatures, the sea itself, and the storms. Therefore she is associated with wrath, revenge, male hatred and the spread of infectious diseases. In some versions Sedna still finds happiness by marrying a sea creature. From her fingers and hands, whales and walruses emerge in different versions of the myth.

Sedna's discovery-horoscope contains the most important indicators for her interpretation. The Sun is conjunct Pholus / Tezcalipoca / Sado / Pandora / Achilles / Virtus / Siegena in 21°27 Scorpio in 4 on the fixed star Unukalhai (*quarrels, exile, unhappy life*) right in opposition to the North nodes on Alu (*making a mess of a situation*) in the 21th degree Taurus. Sedna thus stands for a powerful lightning core that upsets order and closed systems in the face of what has been mapped out as a subcutaneous or karmic destination. Her Sun also makes a square with Asbolus / Machiavelli / Hidalgo (*derailed brutal and dark abuse of power*). North nodes-ruler Venus is inconjunct Saturn. The values of someone with Venus inconjunct Saturn have little or nothing in common with the expectations of society, so there is a strong tendency to ignore them whenever possible, because the prevailing social norms and limitations have no relevance to one's own life. Also money is not considered very interesting, but at the same time one cannot do without it. This inconjunct creates both a subcutaneous field of tension and a creative potential. Neptune, under which the spiritual values reside, is conjunct Damocles (*disintegrate*) and square Crantor (*the end, sudden death, tenderness*), but trine Haumea / Rhadamantus / 2004 EW95 / 1998 XB (*rights for the divine feminine, maternal, accompanied by the visionary and sexual*). Sedna in 17°58 Taurus is conjunct the star Ruchbah (*haughy, proud, but also demanding respect*) conjunct Ophelia (*woman's body lying in the water*); conjunct Colocolo (*never submit to a strong opponent*) opposition Starr (*the glamour girl that should shine*); trine Aletheia / Veritas (*the truth and nothing but the truth*) and Randi / Lust (*lust*); trine Osiris (*rebirth after mutilation*). The discovery Ascendant in 13°19' Leo on Kochab (*the mind that does not conform*) is trine Venus. Mercury is strong and 2007 OR10 is conjunct Uranus (*a stranger in a social group, to incite a revolt*). The conjunction Moon / Hilda / Circe pulls feelings and persona into the dark and builds up female power. Moon is in Cancer sextile Sedna and trine Sun.

Thus we find the Sedna myth underlined in the discovery-horoscope. The core drama and essence of Sedna comes very close to that of the fixed star Algol and the Medusa / Lilith myths and overlaps Black Moon in its resolute refusal aspect. A big difference, however, is the more Water-like nature. Sedna is far more Neptunian than Uranic/Plutonic. It is easier to summarize Sedna in descriptions than in condensed core concepts. Sedna gives an intensely increased awareness of the drama that takes place between macro-, and microcosm, thus the total interaction between celestial bodies and events on Earth. That what the Ancient Greeks called δρᾶμα (drama). Drama simply means *doing*, but meant are the archetypal forces expressing themselves through personalities. Sedna perceives and places, or assesses, these forces. Different cultures dealt with this hyper-awareness in different ways. The Babylonians wanted to be ahead of the whims of the gods by calculating the course and aspects of the planets, and thus they took astrology to an unprecedented height. The Egyptians lost their patience with the annoying moods of the gods and in a Promethean way fused religion with magic in the concept of Heka. By using magical rituals they tried to buffer the difficult aspects of the planets/gods and catalyze the favorable ones. The pre-Hellenistic Greeks chose a more substantial solution: eudaimonism, or the "*pursuit of the happy daemon*" as an attitude to life and goal to pursue.

Every astrologer knows that there are always positive and negative aspects going on, every day, 24 hours a day. However, how the energy of these celestial bodies finds embedding and thus empowerment in current affairs depends to a large extent on the mental state and focus of individuals, the status of a nation, and on the genius loci and modified cultural organization of the civilization in question. For example: the same astrological transits work out differently, because of the foundation charts of nations and their psycho-spheric climate. Western culture solidified in matter and habits, especially the Saturnal and Martial energies and later in the digital world those of Uranus and Neptune. Thus creating "cosmic energy receiving templates" which are not very balanced and which still feed the domination of the left brain hemisphere. Many so called primitive peoples, though infected by the West, have receiving templates that are completely different, making it much easier for right brain hemisphere corresponding energies to condense in the material reality. For a long time the Greeks maintained a relatively harmonious environment and a harmonious social climate based on the balance of left (Neikos) and right (Phile). In such a climate, all energies and associated psycho-spheres can much easier embed and manifest themselves than in a commercialized environment and culture, as is unfortunately the case today.

While I'm writing this, – strongly catalyzed by neoliberalism and American reality making since 9/11 and other PNAC-strategies – the entire Western 21st century reality mode has become a lubricant for especially the negative Saturn, Mercury, Mars and Plutino forces. They are pulled, in a dis-proportionally dangerous way, much more into concrete manifestation than the soft, subtle, human, creative, liberating and life-stimulating influences. Under normal circumstances there are enough positive astrological influences to counterbalance the negative, but "reality" is now designed in such a way that they can barely get through, or are as easily overruled as a swarm of butterflies by a bulldozer. Many astrologers tend to neglect the influence of the *astrological tonus of the embedding or energy-receiving field of our modified reality* and the unbalance this gives between harmonious and harsh astrological forces, in favor of the latter; thus creating a worldwide distortion and darkening in the natural kaleidoscope of macro-microcosmic fluctuations and corresponding influences.

Sedna sees the distinction between World and / Universe, reality and reality modification and no astrologically mapped celestial body so far has such a complete overview of the total, the awareness of being conscious of our own consciousness, while keeping in touch with unspoiled reality, free from artificiality and modification/brainwash by the Media. "*Awake from sleeping, awake from waking*" as Aleister Crowley called it. The revolt of Sedna therefore is a trans-political, trans-cultural revolt, *beyond all isms*. Sedna dares to declare and explain "reality" in terms of mass-psychosis. Strongly aspected and placed in the birth chart or progressed or solar return chart, Sedna can make major contributions to consciousness within the context as depicted above, aspiring a more humane society and more livable planet Earth (here it partly overlaps Haumea).

Yet Sedna can also be quite problematic, because especially the conjunction with the Sun in the radix chart may give so much empathetic and intuitive understanding for people in the environment, that the personal self is never really present, but seems to be somewhere behind the horizon, so that it is also difficult for others to make real personal or intimate contact. The personality gets something fluid, angelic, distant and lonely at the same time. The Moon / Hilda conjunction in the discovery horoscope of Sedna, makes real emotional connection and bonding extra difficult. With a strong Sedna, it can be highly recommended to train self-esteem, to cultivate ones artistic and creative talents, and learn to refuse being swallowed up or infiltrated by the otherworldly or one's own negative contemplation on it. The positive Sedna is sometimes strong in the horoscopes of musicians. Sedna has to ground through the personal and human interaction, even when that seems like a formidable task.

Sedna has a very long and approximate cycle time of approximately 11155 years with a possible deviation of 26 years, which links Sedna's influence to very large and fundamental changes in the Zeitgeist and cultures throughout the ages, and probably also to climate changes and plate tectonics.

42355 TYPHON

fighting your way in; acts of bravery; climatic disasters; typhoons; seaquakes; crowbars

Typhon is a SDO annex Binary Extended Centaur. Typhon was discovered automatically on February 5, 2002, by Near-Earth Asteroid Tracking (NEAT), and is currently estimated at 162 km in diameter. Its moon Echidna was discovered in 2006 and measures 89 km. Echidna orbits Typhon at ~1300 km, completing one orbit in about 11 days, thus forming, together with Typhon, a large object and making it the first discovered binary system within the Centaur class.

In Greek mythology, Typhon, or Typhée (in ancient Greek Τυφάων / Tupháôn or Τυφωεύς / Tuphôeús, from τῦφος / tûphos, "the smoke"), is a primitive evil deity. He is the son of Gaia (the Earth) and Tartarus. According to legend, Typhon is considered to be the Titan of strong winds and storms. However, another tradition (Homeric Hymn to Apollo) rejuvenates him for several generations by making him a demon born of Hera without any male help. Dissatisfied to have seen Zeus give birth to his daughter Athena alone (by devouring her pregnant mother), she would have summoned Gaia, Cronos and the Titans to give birth alone to a male child more powerful than the other gods, and would have been obeyed. This post-hesiodic tradition linked to the Apollo cycle also reports that it is to another monster, the female dragon Python, that Hera entrusted Typhon.

Typhon stimulates: fighting your way in, situations in which one has to prove oneself for the admission; perseverance, ausdauer; intense energy; a hate of control; the dark side, the magical, black magic, a devilish character; emotional shocks, knocking things over, iconoclasm, sex drive, fetishism, disrupting a system or homeostasis; to work yourself up, fighting oneself free from being insignificant, being resolutely ambitious. The positive Typhon acts a bit like a mental/emotional crowbar which can help you to break out of a farce and put you on track again. In the birth chart, on a deeper psychological level, Typhon indicates – by means of especially the conjunctions and oppositions – what we fear to manifest ourselves, or in ourselves, or what we run away from, until the built up tension can no longer be suppressed. Then these displacements tend to manifest themselves as emotional eruptions, which, in a positive way, can act as a prelude to a new phase of life which demands a more complete and authentic existence. Typhon links this to daring to face the monstrous, confronting the monstrous, to wandering through the dark, the risk area, relying only on one's own will and strength (tests of courage). Typhon clarifies the areas of tension between the conditions, needs and requirements for our individuation process and the social obligations to the outside world and keeps on struggling until a balance is reached. "Monsters" are also creative (as they are so wonderfully out-of-the-box). Typhon often increases creativity, daring and originality. Mundane, Typhon is prominent in major disasters (including Fukushima), earthquakes, seaquakes, riots, strikes, rebellion, especially in afflictions by Black Moon, Uranus, and Eris.

The orbital period is 236 years and 256 days.

472235 ZHULONG

Determined diplomacy, diplomacy in tough and complex cases that rely on stamina, expertise and brilliant tactical insight; getting things done by choosing the proper strategic moment after clever preparations; using tactics and diplomacy to start a new phase or process; binding opposing groups, personalities or forces.

On the 27th of August, 2019, (472235) 2014 GE45 was officially named Zhulong. The object was discovered in 2011 and designated 2011 GY61, but the Minor Planet Center, which is responsible for official numbering, considered this to be a pre-discovery. The SDO with an estimated diameter of 233 km was discovered on April 4, 2014 by Pan-STARRS 1 at Haleakala, Hawaii. Zhulong or Zhuyin, also known in English as the *Torch Dragon*, was a giant red solar dragon and god in Chinese mythology. It supposedly had a human's face and snake's body, created day and night by opening and closing its eyes, and created seasonal winds by breathing. It is described in classic Chinese literature as shining a torch over "the nine-fold darkness." The name was suggested by students at the National Dali School.

The key word in the names "Zhuyin" and "Zhulong" is pronounced zhú in present-day Mandarin. It describes the act of "shining" or "illuminating" something. In the Chu Ci, Zhulong is also rendered as Chuolong, which can variously mean "Distant" or "Quarrelsome Dragon", and as Zhuolong, variously "Outstanding" or "Departed Dragon". Zhulong or Zhuyin was not the only serpent-bodied celestial deity in Chinese folklore. Other examples include Pangu, Fuxi, Nüwa and Gonggong. John S. Major describes the Torch Dragon as "well-known in early Chinese mythology" and suggests it is probably "a mythical interpretation of the Aurora Borealis". Others consider it to embody sunlight. Micheal Carr in "*Chinese Dragon Names*" cites a Chinese-language article by Kwang-chih Chang, characterizing it with the Eastern Zhou "Transformation Thesis" that natural elements transform out of the bodily parts of mythical creatures.

At the moment of the official discovery we find Zhulong at 19° 15' Libra in the 3rd house square Rhiphonos in Cancer; conjunct a Mars and Haumea that are in opposition to Eris / 2002 PN34 / Pelion / Spartacus / Weisse Rose / Elst-Pizarro (*one big egoism polluted mess*) in Aries. Zhulong is in very close conjunction to the fixed star Mufrid (*eta Bootis*) or "Star of the Lancer" in constellation Bootis representing the lance he holds in his hand. Sun in the 16th degree Aries is conjunct Uranus, squared by Pluto and opposes the sign Zhulong was discovered in, denoting strong ambitions. Sun is fiery and military, as in conjunction with Taurinensis / Minerva (*clever strategy*) and opposition Typhon (*infighting*). The Moon at 18°31' Gemini is conjunct 2001 SQ73 / conjunct 2002 VE95 / conjunct 1998 WW24 (*continuous pressure fluctuations related to intellectual autocracy and using drugs or alcohol as creative stimulant*) at midpoint from two squares Neoptolemus / Elatus | Colocolo (*the absolute necessity to win or conquer*) opposite Plutino 2001 KN77 (*anger management, Samurai-like self control*). Mercury is exact trine Varuna in Cancer and trine Vertex / 1994 JQ1 in Scorpio or conversely Vertex is conjunct 1994 JQ1 (*decoding, truth seeking*) at midpoint Varuna (*big Media attention*) and Mercury (*communication*). Venus is in the anaretic 30th degree Aquarius and fiery, intellectually pushed by a sextile 1998 HK151 (*word-power, NLP*) / 2001 KF77 (*assertive whistle blowing*) / Amycus (*power drive*) / Hylonome (*popularity*) inconjunct Makemake (*peak performance*). The Mean node and True Node are conjunct with the Mean node trine Venus in the anaretic degree of 30 Libra. The Black Moons in Leo in the first house denote a radical purging of the persona, physical manifestation and self, while refusing all interfering pressure within this process from the outside world.

Thus the raising of a most pure fire is stimulated. This within an overall setting that is clever, intellectual, aimed at active connecting, ambitious, visionary, communicative. Zhulong has no doubt a pulsating and fiery ambitious energy, but this is aimed at diplomacy. Pluto (in Capricorn) and Uranus / Sun (in Aries) square point at the revolutionary element. Zhulong's significance in the chart is centered around diplomacy, diplomacy in tough and complex cases that rely on stamina, expertise and brilliant tactical insight; getting things done by choosing the proper strategic moment after clever preparations; using tactics and diplomacy to start a new phase or process; binding opposing groups, personalities or forces.

In forensic astrology this SDO works very bad for Israel, due to Toro in the discovery chart. The object can further denote a fire that spreads in a line, especially a contra fire, deliberately lit to stop forest fires from spreading further; the "right hand" of a leader; lightning; harmony or joy immediately after a goal has been reached or target has been hit; a goal in football or other sports.

Benjamin Netanyahu has Zhulong conjunct house-cusp 11 / Vertex / 2001 SQ73 / Heracles / Venusia / Dick; square Sun; square osc. Black Moon; semi-sextile Mars; opposite Israel. According to political insiders he was the one who before Rumsfeld and the Neocons first launched the idea for a shock and awe-inspiring "terrorist-attack", which resulted in the 9/11/PNAC swindle and the war mongering that caused so many deaths, Orwellian shit and refugees, serving the full spectrum dominance of the USA, while in Israel he keeps ignoring the barriers of international politics and ethical demands on human rights. Most of the non-Likud public will not give him a like on Facebook, but his tactical diplomatic skills and power are quite phenomenal. Henry Kissinger has Zhulong in 6°56' Cancer in the second house, conjunct the Plutino 1998 HK151 (*word power, tactical use of NLP*) / Ganesha (*overcoming all obstacles*); sextile Venus (*commitment, relating*); trine Rhiphonos (*man or mouse*) / Tezcatlipoca (*evil cunning*) / 2002 VR128 (*higher spiritual and/or apocalyptic awareness*); inconjunct Mors-Somnus in Sagittarius (*works behind the scenes*); inconjunct Menelaus in Aquarius (*scope, challenge*). Mohandas Ghandi, who fought for India's independence of the British and who was opposed to the caste-system and racism, had Zhulong in 10°53 Gemini in the 10th house conjunct Cyllarus (*nationalism, racism*); sextile 2002 AW197 (*super strategy; to put the world upside down for love, harmony and the greater good; world-karma*); opposite the Plutino 1998 VG44 (*official state policy, enforced disinformation*).

The orbital period is ca 420 years and 7 – 25 days.

SDOS & DETACHED OBJECTS WITH ENCODING ONLY IN ORDER OF MPC NUMBER

15874 1996 TL66 (NAME SUGGESTION: GEISER)

Bubbling or cooking until something erupts or discharges; geyser effect; abrupt dramatic change; winning a very large lottery prize; billionaires.

1996 TL66 is a SDO and icy Dwarf planet candidate, discovered on October 9, 1996 by David C. Jewitt, Jane X. Luu, Jun Chen and C. A. Trujillo. The diameter has been estimated by several observatories and gives different outcomes: 575 km (Spitzer Space Telescope) or 339 km (Herschel Space Observatory). 1996 TL66 has been given a very bad name by a number of researchers, but is essentially linked by the Russian astrologer Gennady Maslov to a *breakthrough*, especially the breakthrough or release of energy that was preceded by a period in which the energy was trapped. Via D. Nizhelchenko, 1996 TL66 has been linked to nuclear explosions. Gennady Maslov associates the SDO less dramatically to spraying of a fountain, to lesbians and a breakthrough in one's consciousness, but surprisingly he found 1996 TL66 also strongly positioned in the horoscopes of people who won very large lottery prizes. Mark Andrew Holmes gives as associations for 1996 TL66: putting an end to something; inhuman; ugly; revenging or vindictive; suffering; persecution; destruction; revelation; epiphany; something mystical or apocalyptic; knowing without words; watersheds. Roy MacKinnon associates 1996 TL66 with: "Perception of a new order. Total transformation of understanding. The unimaginable destruction of the holocaust. Direct gnosis, no words. Subtle insight, second sight, clairvoyance. The flash that blinds. Unlimited power. Abuse of power. Mystical revelation of the Divine. The moment of truth. The time warp. Instant new knowledge etched into the soul. The silence that deafens. Precognitive vision. Connection between two worlds, microcosm/macrocosm". John Delaney links 1996 TL66 to: analyzing the part in relationship to the whole; relationship between original structure & eventual evolution; holistic thinking; inability to simplify; diagrams; annotations; footnotes; "grinding mind"; heretic; dissociation from intellectual & religious premises; orthodoxy via discontinuity from origins; traditional severity; from the peripheral to the central core.

Reflecting on the above associations in the discovery chart gives a number of interesting results. First of all, the bad boy image: The discovery-Sun is in minute exact conjunction with the devilish Tezcatlipoca, Pest and Susansmith (*being falsely accused*). 1996 TL66 itself is on the star Sheratan. Conjunct Plutino 2002 VE95 (*drugs and creativity*) and in slightly weaker conjunction with "self-side extremist" Pylenor in the 8th house in Taurus, opposition Tantalus in Scorpio and square Damocles in Aquarius. Roughly conjunct the cusp of the 9th house however, thus in the "anaretic zone" of the 8th house. The 8th house is the house of death, impersonal money, the occult, transformation by unraveling and creating a new homeostasis or self-order. This fact is in line with Maslov, Holmes, MacKinnon and Delaney. The more radical forms of sexual expression belong to the 8th house. Pornstar Cytheria, especially famous for extreme squirt-scenes, has 1996 TL66 strongly characterized in the 5th degree Aries conjunct Pholus / 1998 WA31 / 1995 SM55; opposition Sun / Klotho / Nyx / Dolores in 5 Libra; trine Hylonome / Venusia in 5 Lion; square Industria in 5 Cancer and square Lilith in 4 Capricorn. The name Cytheria means Venus (Venusia) and she became one of the most popular (Hylonome) porn actresses in the world with enormous amounts of ejaculate during her orgasms (*fountains, water streams*). In the discovery chart of 1996 TL66, Venus is "emotionally frustrated" in Virgo on the Ascendant conjunct Logos / Lilith, which is a classic Venus position to become either asexual or to manifest exactly the opposite: the need for extremes in ones love and sex life in order to feel any satisfaction in this life segment. In the 1996 TL66 discovery-chart, Venus has influence over the first, second, third, fourth, seventh, ninth and tenth house. The Water-Element is strongly associated with the discovery-chart and connects this Element with the Cubewano Chaos. 1996 TL66 is often strongly positioned in the charts of porn actors and actresses. This is because of the discharge facet of this Venus impregnated SDO. Unlike, for example, the orgasm/extasy-Centaur 2000 CO104, where the drive is intrinsically an urge for ecstasy sec, the orgasm/discharge in 1996 TL66 is primarily the result of a continuous boiling and bubbling until the pressure on the kettle becomes too high. A small difference with much mutual overlap, but important to notice. Neptune trines Chaos, but also the sea and ocean connected Ceto and makes an opposition with the aqueous Sila-Nunam. All Water-houses have their cusp in a Fire-sign (*boiling, bubbling, spraying geyser effect*). The second house is very richly occupied and is also ruled by Venus. Jupiter is on cusp 5 (*gambling, lotteries*) and Varuna on cusp 11 (*wishes, luck*); square the 2nd and 8th houses.

Interesting is the position of 1996 TL66 in the horoscope of the Dutch NOS-news editor Marcel Gelauff. The NOS television news, like all mainstream news, only has the function of maintaining a consensus on reality that suits government, super industry and CIA, and all so-called "news" is calibrated accordingly. Mainstream news causes constant negative stress and irritation, necessary to maintain a negative economy and fear structure (*bubbling*). Totally different from serious journalism in which finding the truth is the goal. Regularly the indoctrinating of the masses has to come to a boiling point and discharge, to serve international political aims. For example by presenting the many NATO/Gladio attacks as acts of terrorism, Syrian passports included. Gelauff has 1996 TL66 sextile Mercury (*communication*); sextile Sedna (*contemplative distance from the world stage*) opposition 1998 HK151 (*word power, use and misuse of NLP-techniques*) / 2001 SQ73 (*pressure changes*). The cooking pressure can be maintained and increased for a long time at 1996 TL66, because the Moon (*emotions*) is tempered in Virgo in the first house of the discovery-horoscope and Mars (ruler 8) in Leo in 12 makes a sextile with Sun / Asbolus in Libra in 2. This can indeed refer to the successful stock market investor or an investor who can keep his emotions under control and who, under high voltage, is able to wait a long time for the right moment to sell or buy (large). Billionaire Warren Buffet has 1996 TL66 in the first degree Aquarius in the first house conjunct cusp 2nd house, conjunct Thereus / 1995 SM55 in almost minute exact sextile Hylonome / Varuna / Eris in Aries. Millionaire Suleiman Kerimov has 1996 TL66 a.o. conjunct 1998 WU31; square Hylonome opposition 1998 HK151 / 2002 PN34 / Pelion. Billionaire Mihail Prokhorov has 1996 TL66 square Hylonome / Moon in Gemini; square Rhiphonos in Sagittarius; opposition Mars / Uranus / Bienor. Billionaire Harold Simmons has 1996 TL66 conjunct Crantor; sextile Hylonome / Eris / Amycus; square Mercury / Sila-Nunam and opposition Haumea / Deucalion. Billionaire Carl Icahn has 1996 TL66 a.o. conjunct 2003 VS2 / VATT in sextile Hylonome / Amycus / Ceto in Aries; sextile Moon in Sagittarius; trine Black Moon / Okyrhoe; square Sila-Nunam / 2001 BL41; square Elatus. And finally billionaire Alaweed bin Talal Alsaud has 1996 TL66 conjunct the Plutino 1998 US43, right in opposition with Pluto / Haumea / 2002 PN34 / Spirit / Klotho. Interesting, by the way, are the 1996 TL66 – Hylonome contacts here. (In this series on asteroids the examples are based on exact aspects, so within a 1 degree orb, apart from a very few exceptions among the Plutinos.)

The orbital period of 1996 TL66 is 761 years and 256 days.

26181 1996 GQ21

Ambitious pursuit of financial independence; reassessing the value of something; life turning point through paranormal experience; domestic violence; euthanasia; collusion constructions through greed.

1996 GQ21 was discovered on April 12, 1996 by Nichole M. Danzl and measures 401 km in diameter. Characteristics: a passionate ambitious striving, in particular for financial independence; radical resets concerning one's own views on valuations and value judgments; acquiring deep karmic insight through exceptional events of a paranormal nature; communicative work related to art, fashion, aesthetics, relationship mediation or the trade in beauty or care products; being a spokesperson and advocate for the right of committing euthanasia. In extreme cases, an afflicted 1996 GQ21 may indicate a (bloody) violent crime that occurs at home or in the parental home or at the beginning or end of life. In a politician's horoscope, 1996 GQ21 almost always indicates some corrupt behind-the-scenes form of power politics and collusion-constructions, which one continues to expand. The discovery of 1996 GQ21 conjunct the star Foramen indicates that greed is the biggest pitfall here. The field of tension between Aries and Libra energy is maximal with this SDO, so the mine/I versus the us/we-drama is certainly elaborated or emphasized with a dominant 1996 GQ21, in which every form of claiming (or claim a certain behavior of others) must be abandoned, while the art of negotiating and learning to share and work together will prove to be the only way.

The orbital time is 924 years and 99 days.

29981 1999 TD10

Invasions; dealing with invasions; negative or forced fusions; becoming very aware of all invasive and/or parasitical forces and entities; learning to see the weak spot in the defense of a system, building, person or any kind of framework or mind-frame; in negative aspect: becoming the invader; losing sight of ethics regarding other peoples boundaries and privacy.

1999 TD10 is an SDO annex Centaur of 110 km diameter. The object was automatically discovered on October 3, 1999 by Spacewatch. This is a very important SDO, in both personal charts, forensic and mundane astrology. It was discovered, while transiting the 26th degree of Pisces conjunct 1999 TC36 / 2005 UJ438 following Mors-Sumanus (*sensitive, open, metaphysically leading into the dark zone*); trine Typhon (*infighting*) and trine Charybdis / Rhiphonos (*whether or not to be swallowed up in correlation to man-or-mouse dilemmas*). Moon in Gemini is conjunct Izhdubar / Pallas (*opportunistic politics doomed to fail and/or leave a mess*); the Sun is conjunct Crantor / Arachne / Taurinensis (*abruptly deploy or terminate a strategic network*). Furthermore, there is a striking conjunction Varuna/2001 BL41 (*huge abundance in 2*); Mars in Sagittarius is trine Eris / Vinciquerra in Aries (*an extremely focused or even blinding victory mentality which overrules the human factor*); Leviathan trine 1998 US43 (*major political demonisation by means of Media lies*); Machiavelli is conjunct Verdun / Phaeton opposition Chiron (*uncontrolled massacres or bloodshed committed by people, politicians, "systems" drunk with power*) and Jupiter square Neptune (*big illusions, selling the skin of the bear before the bear has been shot, pharmacists*). Asbolus and Nessus are in the 7th house (*public enemies, partners*) with Pluto on the cusp. In plain English, this puts an overload of power play and manipulation in the house of cooperation, partnerships and mutual interest. With 1999 TD10 everything seems to revolve around the concept of invasion, crossing boundaries and in this context the placement in passive houses and signs versus the active houses and signs is of course very important, as it denotes the dilemma "invade or be invaded", psychologically a very paranoid predisposition in both ways.

The concept of invasion can apply to anything, but in the horoscopes of nations it usually refers to suffering from or starting an invasive war or invasion because of multinational interests or other strategically connected powers behind the scenes. Invasion can also refer to contamination with a virus or chemical substance etc... depending on the chart concerned. There is also this earlier mentioned link with abundance, which however rarely shows itself in 1999 TD10, or is stripped bare from the human perception of abundance (*robbery by multinationals*). The state of Israel has 1999 TD10 under high voltage in the first house in Scorpio opposition Nessus in Taurus and square Pluto in Leo. The USA, the country that in the 20th century has invaded almost the entire planet, including world press and world health care and aggressively imposes itself in every possible way (even in the private lives of every world citizen; Echelon, NSA, etc.), has 1999 TD10 in the 9th degree Libra in the 10th house conjunct Eros (*passion*), strongly square Eris in Capricorn (*never criticizing one's own "authority")*; strongly square 1992 QB1 (*no bridging, but imposing culture*); trine Uranus / Gonggong (*justifying invasions under the guise of a right for freedom);* trine Machiavelli and opposition Verdun / Thoreau / Skuld (*causing massacres in every nation that wants an autonomous and US independent government*) and sextile Thereus in Sagittarius (*within this context: air strikes, defying civilization*). Iraq has

1999 TD10 in the 15th degree Scorpio in 4, conjunct the first degree of Via Combusta (*invasions in one's own country*); conjunct Cyllarus (*invasions for ethnic reasons*); opposition Varuna (*getting invaded by a superpower*); square Mercury / Ascendant (*trade*); square 7 (*public enemies*). Anti-Monsanto activist Dr. Vandana Shiva has 1999 TD10 conjunct her Sun in Scorpio. She leads a worldwide protest after already more than 250,000 Indian farmers have committed suicide because of the Monsanto invasion.

Transits of 1999 TD10 in the person's horoscope over (or to) important players such as chart-ruler, Sun, Ascendant or Moon can be extremely unpleasant, even the half sextile aspect comes often accompanied by increased stress, worries and a financial dip. Just like is the case with a strongly afflicted Mars in 12, you can be threatened and have your privacy or economic position attacked in a very cowardly and disruptive way, in which you tend to strongly defend yourself – while it's better to think tactically – to get out of the situation imposed on you. The trick then is not to sit in fear, which alienates you from yourself, and which would be an invasion of your own homeostasis. That is the big booby trap of 1999 TD10. Finding a way to blame the invasion/ infringement on your private or business life sometimes works best through an abruptly initiated measure directly aimed at the opponent's Achilles heel and in such a way that the opponent gives up. 1999 TD10 is usually not an SDO you can ignore when it makes a hard transit (mainly due to the very slow passing time of a 1999 TD10-transit). The degree and house position of 1999 TD10 in the radix horoscope, the progressive and solar return chart, as well as the transits indicate where and when one can be overwhelmed by others with some form of invasion; or vice versa, where one should shed more light on the privacy of others and become more aware of them.

The orbital period is 958 years and 292 days.

40314 1999 KR16

Dissonance between what one wants to propagate and should radiate; sacrifice, renunciation of things; being limited; ascending on the social ladder after self-purification.

1999 KR16 is a Detached SDO of 304 km diameter that was discovered on May 16, 1999 by A. Dalsanti and O. R. Hainaut. Mark Andrew Holmes links 1999 KR16 to limitation and sacrifice and the discovery-horoscope seems to underline this link. 1999 KR16 also has an association with the unlearning or relativizing all kinds of drivel and missionary behavior, as well as failure of what one wants to *convey* for the sake of what one should *radiate* from a point of justified authority; conflicts or dissonances between *propagation* and *radiation* are explicitly covered by this SDO. With a strong 1999 KR16 this dissonance will regularly lead to an inner crisis. Negative Scorpio characteristics are purged towards a "*Don't lie to yourself and get real!*" for a mercilessly long time. The process only ends until the soul is sublimated in this aspect. The discovery of 1999 KR16 conjunct the very favorable star Arcturus paradoxically suggests a very favorable effect and the discovery-Sun is conjunct Priapus (*make things flow easily and abundantly*). 1999 KR16 seems however to keep the brake on full successful development until the last skeletons are out of the closet and, as it were, a radical karmic cleansing has taken place. Like most SDOs, when dominant in the birth chart or becoming dominant due to progressions or major transits this one also can penetrate deep into the soul and ones very being.

The orbital period is 343 years and 22 days.

48639 1995 TL8 (NAME SUGGESTION: HEKA)

Extreme purging and cleaning up of the spiritual consensus; spiritual or occult acts that are revolutionary; occultism XXL; fusion of spirituality with magic (heka); extreme sexual dynamics or risk-taking in order to arrive at complete self-expression; forced relocation or emigration; the constant challenge to take and keep one's own life in one's own hands; seeking radical communication with the subconscious until one's own core identity is solidified.

1995 TL8 is a binary SDO of about 350 km in diameter, with a satellite of 160 km. The object was discovered by Arianna E. Gleason on October 15, 1995. The moon was discovered on November 9, 2002. 1995 TL8 was in 22°20 Aries conjunct the star Baten Kaitos (*forced change*); conjunct the Haumeid 1995 SM55 (*breakthrough, conversion*) / Seraphina (*claiming, bad self control, loves guru's*); opposition Sun; square Neptune / Pelion. Very striking is the super-conjunction Typhon / Moon / Varuna / Black Moon in Cancer in the 12th house and the super-conjunction Thereus / Mars / Ixion / Pluto /Quaoar in the 5th house in the last half-decanate of Scorpio, with Quaoar just in Sagittarius.

Characteristics of 1995 TL8 in the horoscope are: forced changes during life, usually accompanied by forced abandonment of a place to live, forced relocation, emigration; exile; forced change that proves necessary or favorable for the further course of one's life; a miraculous rescue; trials; transcending depression; radical change in the perception of death and the meaning of death; redefining the concepts of heaven and hell; reversal of transcendence oriented spirituality to earthly spirituality and nature worship, transition from right path to left path spirituality, seeking a spiritual revolution; fusion of mysticism with magic (heka); radical purging of the spiritual and religious; drilling through all fake and illusion on a spiritual, metaphysical or magical level; spiritual integrity; magic; magical rituals; occultism; occult development and growth; talent for astrology; shamanic aptitude; positive use of natural psychotropic drugs to accelerate occult and mystical insights; facing humiliations and obstacles; recurring trials; power accumulation; setbacks are met with ingenuity; Saturnal development towards perfection; great sexual dynamics and need for expression; daring to take great risks from time to time; virility; fear of fully expressing one's own strength or virility; deep feeling; great emotional intelligence, but problems with expressing feelings; erasing one's own feelings; not being seen; seeing, understanding and knowledge acquisition of the wounds and blind spots in the world, society and the Zeitgeist; complex or special relationship with a partner who is older; politically engaged, but not politically active in the conventional way; finding original ways or means to heal something; aversion to regular allopathic medicine; wanting to protect young life and children; outraged when seeing children become victims of war, pollution, crime and multinationals.

Mundane: whaling; seawater mixed with blood; shipping disasters; with strong affliction in women's horoscopes increased risk of breast, and uterine disorders; the blind spot or Achilles heel of the homeland or the opposition party in politics; things that are turned inside out by unconscious forces floating to the surface.

The latter aspect appears very cryptic, but can be understood from the 1995 TL8 discovery chart where the SDO was discovered in the 10th house in Aries in the opposite sign of where the discovery-Sun is located. At this position, there is always a striving for the top and ambition linked to such a newly discovered object, where the Sun acts as a kind of MC. However, when the Sun is in the 4th house, the striving for the top in the classical sense changes from a blossoming into a socially striking position towards being in pursuit of a fusion of truth and self-integrity, as a "bottom point" that must first be reached in order to be able to mentally and emotionally "fuel" a new climb, a new trajectory in life. 1995 TL8 *seeks radical communication with the subconscious until its own core identity is solidified.* This explains, besides the super-cluster in the 12th house and the significant Scorpio occupation, the preoccupation of a strong 1995 TL8 with the mystical, occult, psychological and magical. For a dominant 1995 TL8 in the chart, as for most complex objects with a long, slow orbital time, it is true that it will pose major problems or challenges, but 1995 TL8 also has a gigantic potential for inner development in the service of life improvement and process control. *God helps only those who help themselves* is an appropriate credo here. I suggest the name *Heka* for 1995 TL8 because the ancient Egyptian Heka principle stands for an awareness of reality that does not separate spirituality and magic, but merges them from the knowledge that the gods (planetary forces, etc.) randomly pour prosperity as well as misery over man and man has the right to protect himself against the latter. For this the Egyptians used magic, which is nothing else but to generate a "stone in the pond-effect" where the Cosmos had a different course in store. One that was neither useful, nor educational, nor nourishing, but only disturbing. It requires a high degree of occult development in synergy with a deep awareness of what is truly human, as well as an honest rebellion against a dented spiritual consensus, in order to deal with complexity, as condensed in the influence of 1995 TL8.

The orbital period of this newcomer in astrology is 378 years and 314 days.

60458 2000 CM114

Abrupt changes, transformations or terminations; success as a writer.

2000 CM114 was discovered on February 5, 2000 by Marc William Buie. This is a binary detached SDO of about 150 km diameter with a satellite (S/2006) of 110 km. The interpretation points to abrupt, very radical changes, transformations or terminations; originality; a desire for freedom; popularity and great fame as a writer or communicator, especially if the theme is esoteric or mystical or the use of language is very expressive; creative ambition; striving for creative power development (independence). Essential in mobilizing the positive energy of 2000 CM114 is that the objectives are pure, well worked out and that one works purposefully on one thing instead of splintering the energy through enthusiasm for too many different subjects or processes. The use of drugs of the genre that gives an energy boost such as cocaine, speed, Ritalin, or excessive caffeine can work out more harmful than average and, with a dominant 2000 CM114, even dangerous.

The orbital time is 465 years and 256 days.

60608 2000 EE173

Conflict between faith and spirituality, spiritual integrity; abruptly terminated contacts.

2000 EE173 measures 84 km in diameter and was discovered by Wyn Evans, Jane Luu and Chadwick Trujillo on March 3, 2000. The SDO was in the 20th degree Leo conjunct the star Merak, the Plutino Orcus and asteroid Weisse Rose; square 1998 US43 / 1998 WW24 / 1998 WU31. The discovery-Sun in Pisces is conjunct Bowell / Leviathan / Virtus / Minerva; square Pluto in Sagittarius; sextile Saturn in Taurus; trine 2003 AZ84. Venus is conjunct Uranus; square Flammario; sextile 2001 UR163; sextile Chiron. Mercury is opposed with 1988 XB. Mars / 2001 UO18 in Aries opposes Crantor/2000 GN171 in Libra.

2000 EE173 is primarily concerned with religious integrity or spiritual integrity, with spiritual experience versus religious dogma, with the gap between the spiritual and religious or with outright religious conflict. However, even within the religious or spiritual playing field, this SDO can cause all kinds of aberrations, such as a hysterical attitude towards sexuality, precisely because a Venus-Uranus conjunction is a classic among the indicators for homosexuality and transcending sexual inhibitions. In the vast majority of cases, a dominant 2000 EE173 will raise issues of hypocrisy, mostly focused around image/identiy & spiritual/religious dichotomies, within a religious framework or spiritual context. This may even lead to a substantial religious or spiritual reform. The power of Orcus in Leo is always very compelling and the star Merak usually gives more prestige, growth and power during the course of life. Exceptionally, a dominant 2000 EE173 may also denote imprisonment as a result of religious beliefs. Finally, 2000 EE173 may indicate abruptly broken off contacts or relationships.

The orbital time is exactly 353 years.

82155 2001 FZ173

Soft versus hard; speaking or acting at the right time in relation to favorable cause-effect twists or the laws of karma; shyness issues.

SDO with an estimated diameter of about 165 km, automatically discovered by Spacewatch on March 24, 2001, in the 29th degree Virgo conjunct the star Markeb. The interpretation points to a particular sensitivity to soft versus hard; being sensitive to the human emotional reality versus all kinds of rudeness, unethical strategies or financial malpractices or detecting and resisting this; saying something about an injustice or a wrong situation and undertaking something at the proper time in this context, or forsaking it and thereby harming oneself or others; overcoming shyness or suffering from shyness, or experiencing fluctuating extremes in shyness; the relationship between karmic revolutions and saying something, raising something or undertaking something at the right moment; seeing and grabbing favorable opportunities or missing them; the relationship between sensitivity and karma; being philosophically or religiously engaged; a life with many setbacks that ultimately takes a turn in the right direction.

The orbital period of 2001 FZ173 is 809 years and 328 days.

82158 2001 FP185

Overcoming personal fears with a sober mind; alternative medicine; being a pioneer in medicine.

2001 FP185 was discovered by Marc William Buie on March 26, 2001 and has an estimated diameter of 332 km. 2001 FP185 was at the moment of its discovery conjunct Amycus / BAM in the 30th degree Virgo in opposition with 1999 TC36 / Hilda / Apophis in Pisces on the star Sheat. The discovery-Sun and Moon are both in Aries. The Sun is conjunct Vesta / Heracles / 1994 TB. The interpretation seems to point in the direction of overcoming personal fears, of fears for the unknown, fears which have to do with the paranormal; learning to find one's own courage and strength; daring to be yourself, without clinging to– or hiding behind anything; mind over matter; knowing that if one is impeccable and honest, one does not have to fear anything; self control; alternative medicine; being groundbreaking in medicine; medical inventions; reaching ones goal with strength, perseverance and courage.

The orbital period is 3405 years and 135 days.

87269 2000 OO67

Pegasus Syndrome; freedom and improvement of life through a radical change in consciousness and problem relief; radical turning point in life once having developed an authentic or very original scope.

2000 OO67 was discovered on June 29, 2000 by the Cerro Tololo Inter-American Observatory (CTIO) and is both classified as extended Centaur and SDO of about 64 km in diameter with a gigantic long very elliptical orbit. The aphelion is at 1013.50 EA and the perihelion at 20.77 and almost touches the orbit of Uranus. Characteristics of 2000 OO67: an imperfect, unsatisfactory or heavy life, little luck with money and relationships or partnerships until a breaking point is reached through deep insight into the situation and what one really wants in life. The problems are then no longer confronted linearly or through causal relations, but transcended through a radically different perception of one's reality. This is reminiscent of the 1999 movie *Office space*, in which an ICT-employee, who is in a lifeless relationship and does numbing work goes into hypnotherapy, but during the session the therapist suddenly suffers a heart attack and dies. As a result, the employee remains under hypnosis, which gives him a very positive and relaxed self-image. He is no longer disturbed at all by all kinds of problems and situations that were not OK at work, in his relationship or by other problems which previously bothered him. In this totally new mode, his life takes interesting positive turns and he finally merges his true inner being into his everyday life. This sudden problem-solving by simply transcending it (something other than ignoring it or running away from it or going against it) is known as the Pegasus-syndrome. Other features related to a dominantly positioned 2000 OO67 are: a very problematic love life before a breaking point is reached; export of products, export abroad; philosophy; success as a writer; stable personality, sometimes too serious, too conscientious and therefore too inhibited and self-blocking; expansion and great intensity of the emotional life; growth towards emotional satisfaction, a real home and better family ties; chance to become financially very successful in the later phase of life; issues around tax returns or attacks, especially VAT. 2000 OO67 was discovered conjunct the star Enif (*Epsilon Pegasus*) in the first degree Pisces. The "matured" 2000 OO67 occupies itself mainly with matters typical for the axis 4th house – 10th house and the axis 5th house -11th house. These are the playing fields that have the most attention.

The orbital period is calculated at 11760 years and 106 days and is thus even longer than that of Sedna.

91554 1999 RZ215

Creative future-oriented engineering, science fiction, science fiction film set engineering and special effects; help with a dark night of the soul; hunger problems; black-and-white photography; black-and-white thinking and problems caused by this.

1999 RZ215 was discovered by Jane X. Luu and Chadwick A. Trujillo on September 8, 1999 and measures 116 km in diameter. Regarding the psyche, 1999 RZ215 refers to the dark night of the soul, especially one triggered by a partner or life partner because of a farce that irritates this partner. In this case the partner will most likely be of the Scorpio/Pluto kind and the influence of this partner will be fatalistic, but with an honest attitude, usually positive and transforming. The collision of two personalities can make a crucial (karmic) blind spot appear via a new perspective. Drug use can play a positive or negative role in all this. The own imagined goals in life are subjected to a purging process because there is a disturbing blind spot in it. The regaining of one's own authenticity and authority is the ultimate goal of the psychological process inherent in the intrinsic potency of 1999 RZ215. Going beyond black and white thinking can be a central issue in the process. (1999 RZ215 is linked to the understanding of foreign cultures and religions according to transneptunian-astrology.blogspot.com). The "1999 RZ215-effect"manifests itself during strong transits. In such a transitory period, people are also worried more than average about more earthly matters such as their own life base, stocks, declining sales figures, etc. More forensic, this SDO indicates engineering, medical technology; creative future-aware engineering, science fiction, science fiction film set engineering and special effects; assistance to people who have ended up on the fringes, such as vagrants, addicts, ex-prisoners, traumatized persons etc.; the relationship between food and supplies and related confrontational problems due to stupid trends, stubborn mindsets or surreptitious racism; Third World food problems and famines, failed harvests; black and white photography; photos rich in contrast.

The orbital time is 1029 years and 229 days.

118702 2000 OM67

Pre-sublimation; empowerment of super-performance; aircraft taxiing; high ethical-karmic intelligence.

Detached Scattered Disc Object of 201 km – possibly 267 km in diameter, discovered by Marc W. Buie and Susan D. Kern on July 31, 2000. 2000 OM67 works as a peculiar kind of subcutaneous impulse, which in direct involvement with one's individuation process – and the specific actions and achievements to be carried out within it – pulls the brakes until the moment arrives where all kinds of predispositions and qualities necessary for concretizing one's aspirations have matured, to subsequently enter into a powerful targeted dynamic synergy (pre-sublimation). This is a bit like first taxiing an aircraft towards the right position before it takes off. The most fruitful fields of work are authorship, research, publication and engineering. Helicopter view and holistic perceptions merge in this DSDO to converge power; 2000 OM67 gives a total overview; top manager perspective; general instinct to create many sources; expertise; experience, knowledge and material possibilities available for a single project or flow; very long term patience and perseverance, up to lifelong, because this process is linked to intuitive holistic knowing in a karmic setting. 2000 OM67, like Huya, the Lunar nodes-axis and Vertex, has a very direct influence, by way of some sort of subcutaneous pressure, on the pragmatic output of our destination during our current incarnation. The object is further linked to sudden eruptions of spiritual, psychological, sociological or philosophical insight, which makes a rather abrupt break with the then obsolete insight. 2000 OM67 is also related to the legacy of achievements that makes us be remembered after our death. In a sense, 2000 OM67 is a similar, but more complex force than the centaur Bienor (*fame through performance*).

The orbital period is 977 years and 175 days (latest Russian data).

120132 2003 FY128

An irrepressible need to change the consensus, shifting horizons, combined with a good sense of timing.

2003 FY128 is a Detached Object of about 460 km in diameter, automatically discovered by Near-Earth Asteroid Tracking (NEAT) on March 26, 2003. Zodiac location 3°37 Libra conjunct Virtus in the 10th house. 2003 FY128 seems to have an association with the combination of freedom, breaking out, reaching new horizons and extreme science, or – more individually and psychologically – an irrepressible plutonic intelligence aimed at personal freedom or at overcoming the most insurmountable obstacles. Indomitable, sharp, and immune to mass pressure, fake social ethics or trends. 2003 FY128 is a consensus breaker, not deterred by any outside pressure whatsoever, although strategic enough to know exactly when it is the right time to launch something (well prepared). This then goes with a phenomenal power, which cannot be overthrown, but is, in worst case scenarios, smothered by dead weight arguments of the brainless mob, press and/or political and/or scientific consensus. We find a strongly placed 2003 FY128 in the charts of Nikola Tesla, Rupert Sheldrake and Nikita Khrusjtjov.

The orbital time is 351 years and 186 days.

134210 2005 PQ21 (NAME SUGGESTION: XAVIERA)

Sex XXL, porn, sexual predator; psychospheric sensitivity; visual arts; behind-the-scenes diplomacy.

2005 PQ21 was discovered on August 9, 2005 by the Cerro Tololo Inter-American Observatory (CTIO), while conjunct the star Deneb Adige and measures 192 km in diameter. 2005 PQ21 is a highly sensitive, sensual and sexually charged SDO. It includes sex appeal and all kinds of sexual and sensual subtleties, actions and atmospheres; masturbation and porn, orgasm and/or masturbation addiction or frenzy (with asteroid Lust); eroticism; erotic art and photography; anal sex; transformative experiences in relation to sex; sex with attributes; wet dreams; sexual decadence and perversion as well as popularity based on sexuality related expressions or taboo breaches. The interpretation also points to a talent for subtle behind-the-scenes strategy and diplomacy; Zeitgeist sensitivity; psychospheric intelligence; creative talent in the fields of film, photography, visual arts in general; finding out the truth about paranormal phenomena or complexities. Forensically, 2005 PQ21 refers to a drug-using and/or artistic partner; to advertisements for sex products;

porn films and videos; mechanical aids used for sex, such as vibrators, inflatable sex dolls, fucking machines and other sex toys; emancipatory discussions around sex and LHBT-issues; the anatomy and biochemistry of sex; pheromones; sex hormones; sex scandals; behind-the-scenes politicians, diplomats and advisers working according to the consultation economy model ("poldermodel" in Dutch).

The Dutch prostitute, erotic dancer and spy Mata Hari had 2005 PQ21 in the 21st degree Libra conjunct Narcissus (*decadent, erotic*); Swindle (*deception*) and 1999 TD10 / Manwë (*invasion by using mental suppleness*); sextile Uranus; square uncorrected Black Moon. Multi porn-award winner Adriana Chechik has 2005 PQ21 in 8°29 Aquarius conjunct 2001 SQ73 / Sado / Strong; sextile Lust (*sex, lust*)/ Chrisodom (*anal sex, wit*); trine Kytheria (*horny, strong sex drive*); opposition Amycus / Chiron; square Ajax (*feeling one does not get what one deserves*). The popular porn actress, sex emancipator and author of *The Happy Hooker*, Xaviera Hollander, who turned her hobby into her profession, has 2005 PQ21 in the 6th degree Sagittarius conjunct 1995 QY9 / 2000 OM67 (*erupting passion*); sextile Narcissus / 1998 BU48; trine Venus / Pluto; trine Eris / Typhon; opposition Uranus, I suggest the name Xaviera for this SDO, for reasons which may be clear.

The orbital period is 484 years and 183 days.

145474 2005 SA278

Ethics as measured by the human dimension, positioning of one's own will in relation to interests shared with others.

2005 SA278 was discovered on September 27, 2005, by Andrew C. Becker, Andrew W. Puckett and Jeremy Kubica and measures 253 km in diameter. Indication points to a strong Libra / Aries influence with regard to the law; judgment; restoring balance; ethics and the civilized as opposed to the selfish; understanding of the most complex ethical issues; ethics reflected in human reality; positioning of one's own will in relation to interests shared with others; standing up for (balancing) one's own individualization process against the obligations to the collective; the freeing of one's own will by examining the selfish factor and sublimating it to healthy and balanced self-determination and demarcation of self and will. 2005 SA278 has a predominantly positive impact.

The orbital time is 895 years and 256 days.

145480 2005 TB190 (NAME SUGGESTION: STANDING ROCK)

Creating a safe place during a disastrous period; ecological-social grass-root movements that campaign successfully; the five-minutes-to-twelve feeling.

2005 TB190 is an SDO and dwarf planet candidate with an estimated 464 km diameter. The object was discovered on October 11, 2005 by A.C. Becker, A. Puckett and J. Kubica. Characteristics: the emergence and critically assessing itself of a grass-root movement; the collective intuition of having to stand up for a better world and its empowerment through campaigns; hope; success depends on action that is morally clean, keeps its human character and refrains from destructive radicalism (e.g., the actions against the oil pipeline at Standing Rock in 2016/17); the feeling of being able to create a safe place as a group in the middle of an advancing "flood"; Earth Rights; involvement in the ocean environment and protection of whales; ecological/social protest; A sense of urgency in solving (the world's) problems. Forensic: safe havens in the midst of disaster situations; safe dry places during floods.

2005 TB190 is under the favorable influence of the star Skat and was discovered in the 9th degree Pisces conjunct Manwë-Thorondor (*campaigning*). Gonggong (*groups, group consciousness*) in the 30th grade Aquarius opposition Typhon in 30 Leo. The negative properties of Leo and Virgo are purged by this SDO and Aries energy should be kept in balance (*the motivation must remain honest and pure and should not allow gurus and demagogues to take over the movement.*). I suggest the name Standing Rock for this object, for reasons which may be clear from the above context.

The orbital time is 651 years and 251 days.

230965 2004 XA192

Flow management, flow control, flow creation; strategic genius; magical engineering; great energy and stamina once a course has been set; authentic creative power; effective crisis management; being nurtured by Mother Earth; conversion of the old into the new; upgrades; storm.

2004 XA192 was discovered on December 12, 2004 by the Palomar Observatory and was in the 19th degree Gemini, conjunct the star Hoedus II – one of the two Haedi (*young billygoats, traditionally associated with storm*), conjunct the asteroid Taurinensis (*master strategy*) and the Plutino 2001 YJ140 (*cut the crap*) opposition Zephyr / Summanus (*dark weather, gothic sensuality*). The Sun was conjunct Dimitrov / Industria / Rockefellia in the 4th degree Capricorn; sextile

Uranus / Borasisi in Pisces; sextile Deucalion / Skuld in Scorpio (so on a magic midpoint); trine Electra / Tezcatlipoca in Virgo; trine 2002 VR130 / 1995 SM55 / 2001 SQ73 / 1995 TL8 in Taurus; opposition Swift / Tjelvar. The core of 2004 XA192 seems to be a stormy, magical one, fed by creative turbulence and fluctuating pressure of *1995 SM55 / 2001 SQ73* with a stable centre of gravity from Industria in Capricorn, between "cash flow management asteroid – Rockefellia" – and "crisis management asteroid – Dimitrov". Furthermore (also considering the rest of the discovery-chart) there is a great urge for freedom, with a Mercurial touch and a razor-sharp strategic talent.

Characteristics: flow management, flow control, flow creation; strategic genius; magical engineering; great energy and stamina once a course has been set; authentic creative power; independent knowledge and systematization; effective crisis management; fed by the Earth; the "dissolving or evaporating" of a mainstream trend or a system or organ that has become sluggish and replacing the basis with something new and better; the transformation of the old into the new, or structural renewal of the old; substantive upgrades; a creative output that suddenly takes up its own large terrain – which had previously been invisibly left fallow. Mundane 2004 XA192 will point to a form of gurgling, smothering riots, underground growth processes, underground (r)evolution; stormy weather; something that can – with the right aspects – suddenly become manifest and cannot be ignored by the prevailing consensus.

The orbital period is 324 years and 160 days.

308933 2006 SQ372

Ethics; humanitarianism; assessing legislation and treaties that could damage ethics, the environment, national interest, humanity and/or human values. To counteract on, or contrarily, to impose certain laws or treaties concerning the areas mentioned above.

2006 SQ372 is a Neptune intersecting SDO/Extended Centaur of an estimated 110 km in diameter. The object was discovered by A. C. Becker, A. W. Puckett and J. Kubica on September 27, 2006. At the discovery moment 2006 SQ372 it was conjunct the star Nashira and the asteroids Young and Circe in the 22nd degree Aquarius; opposition Saturn. The Aphelion is at 1570 AU and the Perihelion at 24155 AU. The characteristics of 2006 SQ372 seem to relate to the kind of problems brought under public attention by politicians like Nigel Farage and other opponents of treaties such as the TTIP etc. (*crippling of democratic rights by overruling them with transnationalist and/*

or corporate litigation); testing legislation against ethics and human values; humanitarianism; to counteract on environmental and national interests that are damaging to legislation and treaties or, on the contrary, wanting to impose them; combating racist or nationalistic forms of political extremism. Conversely, in a very negative chart, 2006 SQ372 can act as a catalyst for undemocratically imposing laws, like TTIP etc. The coin always has two sides. Nigel Farage has 2006 SQ372 in the 12th degree Scorpio in the 3rd house conjunct 1999 XX143 (*provocation*) sextile Ascendant / Pluto / Deucalion (*powerful, almost magical personal defense*): trine Orcus / Bowel (*demanding strong integrity*); trine cusp 7th house (*partners, public enemies/treaties*); opposition AMOS (*human perspective).*

The orbital period around the Sun is no less than 32347 years.

523622 2007 TG422

Intensifying sex and/or eroticism; erotic photography, erotic art, eroticism and sex as a field of creative expression combined with ambition; erotic or sexual tattoos; negative: nationalism or in extreme cases racism, aggressive graffiti, "Blut und Boden"; invasion issues; wild, untamable, dark, raw, gothic; prone to accidents.

2007 TG422 is a trans-Neptunian object on a highly eccentric orbit in the scattered disc located in the outermost region of the Solar System, approximately 260 kilometers in diameter. It was discovered on October 3, 2007 by astronomers Andrew Becker, Andrew Puckett and Jeremy Kubica during the Sloan Digital Sky Survey at Apache Point Observatory in New Mexico, United States. According to American astronomer Michael Brown, the bluish object is "possibly" a dwarf planet. It belongs to a group of objects studied in 2014, which lead to the proposition of the hypothetical Planet Nine. Planet Nine is a hypothetical planet in the outer region of the Solar System. Its gravitational effects could explain the unusual clustering of orbits for a group of extreme Trans-Neptunian Objects (eTNO's); bodies beyond Neptune, that orbit the Sun at distances averaging higher than 250 times that of the Earth. These eTNO's tend to make their closest approaches to the Sun in one sector, and their orbits are tilted in a similar way. These improbable alignments suggest that an undiscovered planet may be shepherding the orbits of the most distant known Solar System objects. 2007 TG422 orbits the Sun at a distance of 35.5–910 AU once every 10279 years and 9 months (3,754,688 days; semi-major axis of 473 AU). Its orbit has an exceptionally high eccentricity of 0.92 and an inclination of 19° with respect to the ecliptic.

At the moment of its discovery 2007 TG422 was in 15°20 Taurus conjunct Thereus / 1996 TQ66 square Damocles. Venus in 27 Leo was trine Pluto in 27 Sagittarius / Galactic Center and trine 2001 UR163 in 27 Aries. Moon is in Cancer and the discovery-Sun in Libra conjunct Lust / Pandora trine 1999 TD10 (*invasion*) and opposition 1996 TO66 (*obscene*) / 1995 QY9 (*passion*).

2007 TG422 is a complex SDO. Strongly placed in the birth chart, progressed- or Solar Return chart or during longer transits within a half degree orb, the newcomer can indicate: the intense, a force that intensifies the sexual and/or erotic; erotic photography or film, erotic art, eroticism and sex as a field for creative expression combined with ambition; erotic or sexual tattoos; capable of brilliant synergy of thinking in both text and images, literary imagination; converting the visionary in the textual and vice versa; expecting to get "last minute fame" for ones creativity; wild, untamable, very strong; dark, raw, dirty sex, dark passions. Negative: nationalism or in extreme cases racism, aggressive graffiti, "Blut und Boden"; invasion issues; accident risk; explosion risk; the obscene or ugly.

2007 TG422 Can build up an enormous strength but this strength depends very much on conservation of one's own energy and dealing with the weak spot: invasive elements in one's love or sex life due to the vulnerability that always comes with loving someone very passionately. With the Black Moons in Libra and Scorpio – matrimonial or relational tensions related to passion, honesty, sharing things, working together and sex are intrinsic with a dominant position in the chart of this eSDO. In order to bring forward the more positive energy of this object and to eliminate the invasion aspect as much as possible, it is advisable to wear a chain of snowflake obsidian or snowflake obsidian in the trouser pockets. This stone has very strong anti-invasion properties. This tip also works for 1999 TD10 and the Centaur 2002 PN34!

Forensic: health issues concerning the joints, bones, teeth; chronic or lethal diseases, cancer, health problems due to the hardening of tissue or cold; electrocution, water related or during travels or long transport; fierce media-propaganda that led to legitimatizing the war crimes in Bagdad by USA and NATO.

The orbital period is 10279 years and 78 days.

DAMOCLOIDS, RETROGRADE OBJECTS & (EX)COMETS

5335 DAMOCLES

A nervous feeling of threat, the radical breaking down of a closed system.

Damocles was discovered on February 18, 1991, by Robert H. McNaught. The object measures about 10 km in diameter and the extremely elliptical orbit has an inclination of over 62°. The most impressive historical event which features Damocles as the protagonist is perhaps the disintegration of the Soviet Union. The USSR was founded by conglomerating 15 states into one, on December 30, 1922, with the Sun in 8°16'54 Capricorn. When on December 25, 1991, the USSR and its 15 post-Soviet states collapsed, Damocles at that precise moment accelerated in its transit over the birth Sun of the USSR, assisted by the asteroid Split. Damocloids generally have a disruptive effect on closed systems, thereby dispersing the separate parts that formerly held the system together. So the disintegration of the once largest country in the world coincided with the moment when Damocles, from which the group takes its name, merged with the core of Soviet Russia.

Psychologically speaking, the word anxiety fits best with Damocles as its main characteristic. In the discovery-chart of Damocles the object itself is in the 11th degree Scorpio; sextile Uranus in Capricorn (out-of-the-box visions concerning the official system or status quo); trine Pholus in Cancer (first Domino stone that falls); square Crantor / Orcus (abrupt and definite termination) in Leo. The discovery Sun is in the 29th degree Aquarius trine Chariklo (future); square Quaoar / Thule / Arawn (a growth system that has become elusive for itself and isolates itself more and more); trine Skepticus in Libra (critical of treaties and mutual tolerance) and opposition Sedna (the immense that is beyond active control). The Sun is conjunct Dionysus and 2001 OG298 (wild, extreme power crisis or coup). Pluto is conjunct Varda (eruption of the urge to make a deep impact); Mars in Gemini opposition Toro in Sagittarius (abrupt outburst of violent idea(l)s or goals). The chaos or creation of another order caused by Damocles has something magical and elusive, partly due to a "super-Deucalion" in the discovery-horoscope, connected with Typhon, Nessus, Eris, Neptunus, Nemesis and Sethos, among others.

Damocles-transits always cause unrest and put things in jeopardy. In the radix chart, Damocles gives indications via placement in sign, house and aspecting (especially the conjunction) where, how or why one tends to disturb something or make others nervous in which area or in which facet of life; or vice versa, how others or circumstances assert a disturbing influence. Whether Damocles' energy works outward or inward will primarily depend on active house/sign – passive house/sign combinations and secondarily on aspects.

The orbital period is 40 years and 275 days. A special feature of Damocles' orbit is that for years in a row this object hangs around in the signs Aquarius and Pisces and then suddenly runs through the other signs of the Zodiac with ever increasing speed towards the opposing signs, which he passes very quickly. This weird pattern (common – in many varieties – to most of the Damocloids and retrograde objects) is due to Damocles' extreme inclination of 61.88 degrees.

EPHEMERIS DAMOCLES

01 Jan 2017 | 21 aq 36
01 Jan 2018 | 22 aq 16
01 Jan 2019 | 22 aq 58
01 Jan 2020 | 23 aq 43
01 Jan 2021 | 24 aq 34
01 Jan 2022 | 25 aq 27
01 Jan 2023 | 26 aq 26
01 Jan 2024 | 27 aq 31
01 Jan 2025 | 28 aq 50
01 Jan 2026 | 0 pi 20
01 Jan 2027 | 2 pi 12
01 Jan 2028 | 4 pi 43
01 Jan 2029 | 8 pi 37
01 Jan 2030 | 16 pi 2
01 Jan 2031 | 22 ar 31
01 Jan 2032 | 2 sa 12
01 Jan 2033 | 15 cp 56
01 Jan 2034 | 25 cp 28
01 Jan 2035 | 0 aq 9
01 Jan 2036 | 3 aq 9
01 Jan 2037 | 5 aq 23
01 Jan 2038 | 7 aq 4
01 Jan 2039 | 8 aq 28
01 Jan 2040 | 9 aq 39
01 Jan 2041 | 10 aq 45
01 Jan 2042 | 11 aq 41
01 Jan 2043 | 12 aq 33
01 Jan 2044 | 13 aq 21
01 Jan 2045 | 14 aq 9
01 Jan 2046 | 14 aq 51
01 Jan 2047 | 15 aq 32
01 Jan 2048 | 16 aq 11
01 Jan 2049 | 16 aq 51
01 Jan 2050 | 17 aq 27
01 Jan 2051 | 18 aq 3
01 Jan 2052 | 18 aq 39
01 Jan 2053 | 19 aq 17
01 Jan 2054 | 19 aq 53
01 Jan 2055 | 20 aq 29
01 Jan 2056 | 21 aq 7

20461 DIORETSA

The unusual or extraordinary; gateway to or point of contact with the paranormal; time inversions; déjà-vu moments.

Dioretsa measures about 14 km in diameter and was on June 8, 1999 the first discovered asteroid with a retrograde orbit. Besides the fact that Dioretsa (the name comes from asteroid spelled backwards) runs retrograde, she also has an inclination of 160.4 degrees.

Dioretsa seems to indicate: the unusual, abnormal and extraordinary, in positive aspects linked to the exceptional, creative and mind-expanding. When she makes or receives negative aspects, however, Dioretsa can denote the frustration or blockage of these qualities. Dioretsa is also associated with anachronisms; strange coincidences in experiencing time; order reversals in routine processes; the paranormal, a point of contact with the paranormal, gates to the paranormal or to an another reality, such as the Bardo, astral world, etc.. In this respect, interesting effects could be achieved with psychotropic plants or mushrooms during positive transits from asteroid Datura to Dioretsa or vice versa, as well as in dreams, when Dioretsa makes contact with Somnium, Mors-Sumanus, Altjira or Hypnos. Dioretsa also has to do with turning points in one's life as a result of a special event; with a suppressed talent or ability that is strong, but kept inert due to circumstances; with a devilish kind of energy (in the positive sense of finally freeing our true will: cut the crap, don't be a pussy and just go for it!); with everything that breaks through a fixed or normal pattern. Presumably Dioretsa also has a link with natural portals to other worlds such as ley-lines and ley-line vortexes.

Alfred Watkins (Early British Trackways, Moats, Mounds, Camps and Sites – 1922, The old straight track: its mounds, beacons, moats, sites, and mark stones – 1925 and The Ley Hunter's Manual – 1927) had Dioretsa, at – 6 minutes – exactly conjunct Sedna in the 28th degree Pisces and within a half degree conjunct Cerberus (underworld, the beyond, boundary between the world of the living and the dead). Raymond Andrews associated Dioretsa with code breaking, cryptography, puzzles and learning difficulties. Nikola Tesla had a strongly aspected Dioretsa / 2003 CO1-conjunction. In Pisces, Scorpio and Aquarius the paranormal will most easily emerge. Finally, there is a substantial link between Dioretsa and astrology (discovery-Sun trine Uranus / Utopia / Psyche / Pelion & Discovery and the discovery-Dioretsa conjunct Urania. Finally there is a relation with the déjà-vu phenomenon and – just like other retrograde objects – a link with the Lunar node axis, in which they behave a bit like a kind of routers in the karmic network. Unlike Damocles or Hidalgo, with Dioretsa I have always found the unusual in connection with a generally fascinating use of "perspective is everything" and not with the extreme messing up of a closed system or the undermining of any form of control.

The orbital period is 116 years and 327 days, of which Dioretsa remains about 4 years in Gemini, 17 years in Taurus, 65 years in Aries, 14 years in Pisces and 4 years in Aquarius, before completing the journey through Capricorn, Sagittarius, Scorpio, Libra, Virgo, Leo and Cancer in about 12 years.

65407 2002 RP120

Mind control; brain-hacking; manipulation of mind or memory; memory erasure; brainwashing; MK-Ultra-like crimes; understanding the other's thoughts.

2002 RP120 is a retrograde Damocloid annex SDO, measuring 14.6 km in diameter, which was discovered on September 4, 2002 in the 11th degree Gemini conjunct the "military" star Aldebaran; conjunct Hilda (*energy manipulations, painful conversion processes, extremely sensitive, Plutonic, vampire-like*) opposition Quaoar (*unfolding of large growth and development constructions*) / 2002 KY14 (*disabling someone; working with electrons; unstable course or situations, intellectual study*); square Anga / Pandora / Bienor in Virgo (*becoming familiar with the revelation of malignant, unethical medical matters*); trine Amycus / Beowulf in Libra (*harsh extrusion of the other's identity*). 2002 RP120 made a sextile with Typhon (*infighting*) in Leo and 1998 TB / 2002 TX300 in Aries (*screening the individual by means of a very gross invasion of privacy*) and was also at their midpoint, where Typhon was conjunct with Rockefellia (*big money as a motive*).

The characteristics of 2002 RP120 are: mind control; manipulation of the mind or memory; erasing the memory or putting things in it that do not belong there; brainwashing; MK-Ultra-like crimes; Facebook's Building 8 brain-reading experiments; understanding the thoughts of the other. With strong or many transits from other objects to 2002 RP120 in the radix chart everyone – at certain moments in their life – most likely has to deal with a situation where someone else imposes a totally different version of reality or of an event – or how this event is stored in your memory – than the one you observed yourself. In the radix chart 2002 RP120 also indicates where (determined by, sign, house etc.) you may expect to observe or experience some form of mind fuck, obsession (which works as a blind spot or mental/ emotional prison) mind manipulation, hysterical trend in others or something you always had an aversion to.

When the official research report on the CIA-brainwash project MK-Ultra was published on August 3, 1977, 200 RP120 was in the 28th degree Libra conjunct Jabberwock / Sisyphus (*tormenting repetition of something monstrous using a binding factor*); trine Jupiter in Gemini (*declassified information*); sextile Rhadamantus (*legal affairs*) square Orcus (*integrity assessment*); opposition Cruithne (*birth-ground x nationality vs. identity*). MK-Ultra is diametrically opposed to the media nurtured image of "freedom, democracy and civilization" that America (in vain) likes to maintain – especially since it took place within America's own borders during the Cold War. In the NSA's founding chart (with the CIA as its primary operational tool), 2002 RP120 goes stationary in the phase of closing a retrograde period (i.e. at its strongest) that very day (26 July 1947) in the second degree Scorpio. The object is conjunct 1999 OY3 / Chiron; opposition Hylonome; inconjunct Burney in Gemini; square Sun in Leo; sextile Mors-Somnus (being (in)famous for digging underground to trace who is in contact with whom through gross interrogation methods or infiltration into someone's communications, trade or travel behavior, that the government officially doesn't know anything about – with this very situation acting as the governments very own wound and blind spot). Conscientious whistleblower Edward Snowden has 2002 RP120 conjunct AMOS (*loving; social, strict, visionary/prophetic; soul intelligence; shepherd of the herd*) / Pluto / Saturn (*serious, fatal and substantial responsibility burden or guilt complex with regard to power issues*) and 2002 KX14 (*dealing with criticism*).

EPHEMERIS
2002 RP120

08 Jul 1947 | 1 sc 35 Rx
09 Jul 1947 | 1 sc 34 Rx
10 Jul 1947 | 1 sc 34 Rx
11 Jul 1947 | 1 sc 34 Rx
12 Jul 1947 | 1 sc 34 Rx
13 Jul 1947 | 1 sc 33 Rx
14 Jul 1947 | 1 sc 33 Rx
15 Jul 1947 | 1 sc 33 Rx
16 Jul 1947 | 1 sc 33 Rx
17 Jul 1947 | 1 sc 33 Rx
18 Jul 1947 | 1 sc 33 Rx
19 Jul 1947 | 1 sc 32 Rx
20 Jul 1947 | 1 sc 32 Rx
21 Jul 1947 | 1 sc 32 Rx
22 Jul 1947 | 1 sc 32 Rx
23 Jul 1947 | 1 sc 32 Rx
24 Jul 1947 | 1 sc 32 Rx
25 Jul 1947 | 1 sc 32 Rx

26 Jul 1947 | 1 sc 32 Rx
The NSA was established exactly the same day 2002 RP120 became stationary

27 Jul 1947 | 1 sc 32
28 Jul 1947 | 1 sc 32
29 Jul 1947 | 1 sc 32
30 Jul 1947 | 1 sc 32
31 Jul 1947 | 1 sc 32

2002 RP120 has an extreme orbit. In 6 years the signs Virgo, Leo, Cancer, Gemini, Taurus, Aries, Pisces and Aquarius are traversed. 2002 RP120 transits Cancer in just 22 days and then stays in Scorpio for more than two centuries. The inclination is 119.1 degrees and the orbital period is 405 years and 164 days.

127546 2002 XU93 (NAME SUGGESTION: SERPENT EYE)

Hyper-consciousness; Adam Kadmon; the adversary; being destroyed by the forces of the prevailing mode of reality or chronically in conflict with them ; magical genius; experiencing creation errors; Luciferian drama.

2002 XU93, classified as both (extended) Damocloid and SDO, was discovered on December 4, 2002 by Marc W. Buie. It measures 167 km in diameter and has an inclination of 77.9°. While orbiting, the object remains exceptionally long in the signs Sagittarius and Capricorn. 2002 XU93 was discovered conjunct Sun / Moon / Nocturna / Kama / Solidarity in the 13th degree Sagittarius conjunct the star Alwaid (Rastaban); opposition Dioretsa / 1994 VK8; trine Typhon / Kafka in Leo; trine Black Moon / 1992 QB1 in Aries. Rastaban, the ancient Hebrew name for Alwaid, is located in the eye in the head of the constellation Draco and means Eye of the Subtle Serpent. 2002 XU93 itself was during the discovery in 1°22 Cancer at midpoint (from squares) Narcissus / Shadow (self reflection)|1999 TC36 (metaphysics) ; trine Mars / Juno / Achilles / Sisyphus in Scorpio; sextile 1995 TL8 / 1995 SM55 in Taurus.

Like several other distant objects described in this book, 2002 XU93 seems to perceive reality as a generally unfortunate match between a natural and human reality on one side and a modified or system-reality on the other side, by which it is clearly understood on what basis and on which conceptions this modified reality is constructed, continued, by what means and for which purpose or in whose interest. At the same time, there is a perception of certain concealed motivations behind these apparently human conceptions, which are not human at all, but rooted in energy predatory forces, constructs or entities. As a result, 2002 XU93 is not a primarily political or religious player, although 2002 XU93 when afflicted may express itself politically in extreme ways, but only as a kind of lightning strike, which is considered necessary at that moment and not as a long term hobby. 2002 XU93, if dominant or very strong in the radix horoscope and with sufficient back-up of supporting aspects of other objects, enters into a kind of conflict with the forces of creation themselves, which can be observed behind the scenes of the human stage, together with their infiltration of this human stage and the, unnoticed by others, ruining impact on one's own private life. The perspective of 2002 XU93 is like that of Adam Kadmon, the primordial human and the intuitive humane holistic knowing. This perspective cannot be influenced or corrupted, but remains absolute.

Characteristics: hyper-consciousness; the opponent; being destroyed by the forces of the prevailing mode of reality or chronically in conflict with them;

very heavy and hard opposition by astral guards; magical genius; experiencing errors in the divine creation; wanting to effect a fusion of magic and spirituality; Promethean or Luciferian character; hyper-consciousness as a source of suffering and isolation; misunderstood by the masses and intelligentsia; courageous; sacrificial; visionary; a repeatedly occurring fruitful struggle with the life partner as a result of the above themes and dramatics; being forced to regularly reset and maintain one's own energy field.

Forensic: Zeitgeist changes; (bomb)attacks on high-ranking figures in politics or religion for partly political motives; psychoses. 2002 XU93 should purge the negative qualities of Aries and Taurus to sublimate the positive and focus on simple communication. That is to say, to translate the kind of very useful and complex scopes that one can handle with a strong 2002 XU93 in such a way, that they become comprehensible to a larger public. I suggest the name Serpent Eye for this object because of the discovery position on Rastaban and the inherent Luciferian drama of 2002 XU93.

The orbital period is 549 years and 146 days.

154783 2004 PA44

A tremendous potential, both suffocated and stimulated to develop until the period of manifestation starts; a dream or ideal that is not given up but keeps smoldering, even when one's current incarnation does not find a way to make it come true; learning or training to become capable of managing an overwhelming complexity; prolonged high spiritual, philosophical or literary ambitions or the dream to settle abroad; sensitive to the genius loci of a huge system, process or Zeitgeist and in the end able to translate its nature and course in words and logic; destroys the heart of a suffocating system when it's getting or taking the chance; enforced purification of both mind and feeling, rational and emotional life.

2004 PA44 is both classified as Unusual Object and Damocloid. The object measures 8.4 km in diameter and was, after previous automated observations, discovered by NEAT at the Palomar Observatory, California, on August 7, 2004. The inclination is just 3.4 degrees, which is unusually low for a Damocloid.

When this object is dominant (in very narrow aspects within a 1° or ¾° orb) it can contribute to medium-ship and all Neptunian kinds of creativity or artistry like video, photography, film, music. This will however not manifest when the general composition of the chart is not helpful. In that case what remains are an extreme sensitivity which takes years to get a grip on, a tremendous potential both suffocated and stimulated to develop until the period of manifestation starts; a dream or ideal that is not given up but keeps smoldering, even when in one's current incarnation one does not find the way to make it come true; learning or training to become capable of managing an overwhelming complexity; prolonged high spiritual, philosophical or literary ambitions or the dream to settle abroad; staying sensitive to the genius loci of a huge system, process or Zeitgeist and in the end being able to translate its nature and course in words and logic.

In a very martial chart: an urge to destroy the heart of a suffocating system when it's getting – or taking – the chance; a psychology career. The discovery-chart shows a strongly Neptunian nature, a boiling water aspect via its Moon-aspects: conjunct 1996 TP66 (*decoding*) / 1999 TD10 (*invasion*) / 1996 TL66 (*eruption after cooking point*) / Sedna (*in isolation seeing the whole picture*) / Nocturna (dark) / Cruithne (*birth ground*) / Sundsvall (*genius loci sensitivity*) opposition Ginevra (*female Ghosts*) / Augias (*filth*); square Typhon (*infighting*); sextile Asbolus in Pisces (*dark occult*) – its Pisces-Ascendant (*sensitive, dreamy*) – Sun opposition Neptune / Damocles and a complex creative affinity (Sun in Leo – Neptune in Aquarius). Pluto on the Sagittarius MC (*power lift*) is as the epicentre of a Yod formed by Moon in Taurus conjunct and Saturn in Cancer. Pluto / MC in Sagittarius sec, Sun in Leo, Mars in Leo conjunct 1998 BU48 and Jupiter / Makemake trine Moon form a welcome counterpoint to the sensitive and watery foundation.

2004 PA44 keeps hidden, deep inside, a tremendous and exceptional visionary potential which may or may not come to – sudden – fruition after a long maturing process of one's mind, emotions and intuitive knowing (zoe noesis). This totally depends on the chart as a whole. The object can catalyze both the positive and negative (of the Neptunian / 12th house / Pisces kind e.g. illusions, inability to materialize, letting one's life pass by while staying uninvolved, thus missing all opportunities). The process (Scorpio) should work out, by not getting stuck in the process itself, but striving for a solid homeostasis in life (Taurus), after the old actuality of one's being is purged and the true vision and knowledge is released to ignite the creative flame. In forensic astrology 2004 PA44 can denote: that what is done offline or grows behind the scenes, until public release. In a female chart 2004 PA44 can stimulate a woman's femininity and independence and/or make her a femme fatale, or the opposite; hinder or ruin her femininity.

The orbital period is 53 years and 205 days.

330759 2008 SO218

To generate money resources in relation to a crisis; out-of-the-box perspective on money; underground alternative money/payment systems; bit-coins and crypto-currency; crypto-currency traffic via dark net; black market activities.

2008 SO218 is a retrograde Centaur. The object was automatically discovered on September 30, 2008, by Mt. Lemmon Survey. 2008 SO218 has a primary link with the release of money flows after or during a crisis situation, creating alternative means of payment in a very original or unusual way, out-of-the-box viewpoints on money; local coins and especially the bit-coin and bit-coin transactions via dark net; underground financials.

Other features: breakthrough; financial breakthrough; crude sense of humor; the powerful loner; someone who makes an impact with an action that causes a stir, but who will generally be welcomed. Typical for 2008 SO218 is seeing money for what it really is, right across all financial systems, money experts, rules and habits, namely nothing more or less but an agreement dictated by people with an undeserved authority over money. Three million children die of starvation on this planet every year, for example, simply because of this agreement. All other arguments are utter nonsense, maintained by a very well-organized system of stupidity enforcement, to maintain an exploitation system and defend themselves against more humane visions in a very violent (but bankers and multinationals friendly) way. 2008 SO218 makes one very aware of the dark sides of the money system, but, depending on the overall chart condition, one can just as well dive right into it.

The inclination is 170.3 degrees and the orbital time is 23 years and 47 days.

EPHEMERIS 2008 SO218

30 Sep 2008 | 14 ge 36 Rx
30 Sep 2009 | 11 ar 4 Rx
30 Sep 2010 | 23 cp 32 Rx
30 Sep 2011 | 16 sa 59 Rx
30 Sep 2012 | 27 sc 22
30 Sep 2013 | 14 sc 22
30 Sep 2014 | 4 sc 38
30 Sep 2015 | 26 li 48
30 Sep 2016 | 20 li 11
30 Sep 2017 | 14 li 16
30 Sep 2018 | 8 li 51
30 Sep 2019 | 3 li 45
30 Sep 2020 | 28 vi 54
30 Sep 2021 | 24 vi 4
30 Sep 2022 | 19 vi 13
30 Sep 2023 | 14 vi 16
30 Sep 2024 | 9 vi 8
30 Sep 2025 | 3 vi 34
30 Sep 2026 | 27 le 27
30 Sep 2027 | 20 le 27
30 Sep 2028 | 12 le 4
30 Sep 2029 | 1 le 17
30 Sep 2030 | 15 cn 56 Rx
30 Sep 2031 | 19 ge 50 Rx
30 Sep 2032 | 21 ar 14 Rx
30 Sep 2033 | 29 cp 58 Rx
30 Sep 2034 | 20 sa 20 Rx
30 Sep 2035 | 29 sc 39
30 Sep 2036 | 16 sc 16
30 Sep 2037 | 6 sc 20
30 Sep 2038 | 28 li 22

336756 2010 NV1

A moving away from the "violent", harsh criticism and the bad tempered because of a heightened karmic instinct, and growing towards self-responsibility, which sets in motion a new course of life.

2010 NV1 was discovered by the Wide-field Infrared Survey Explorer (WISE) on July 1, 2010, in the 12th degree Aries and was at the time of its discovery conjunct 2002 KY14 (*to make someone shut up or eliminate the person*). 2010 NV1 is a high inclination retrograde Centaur with a comet-like orbit and measures 44.20 km in diameter with an inclination of 140.8 degrees.

Characteristics: switching off, leaving a karmic pattern; moving away from the destructive, hot tempered, violent, overly critical; growing towards one's own sense of responsibility; curbing destructive passions; an instinctive karmic contact and consciousness that still has psychospheric memories of the consequences of derailment in a previous incarnation. Aspects in the radix horoscope, especially the conjunctions, are triggers of this kind of sensations. Specifically, 2010 NV1 emanates a moving away from the violent and arrogant, towards soul balance. Simultaneously it urges one towards soul balance/reconstruction, that will at some point effect a whole new course of life and a new perspective on life (Uranus at the Aries-point in the discovery horoscope). This wonderful object emanates a very benign influence! Though not spiritual by itself, it exerts the necessary force to reconnect the soul with the true spiritual dimension.

The (heliocentric) orbital period is 5593 years and 332 days.

342842 2008 YB3

Transpersonal intelligence; humane versus destructive technology; progressive reactionary with a "back to nature" accent.

2008 YB3 is a retrograde high inclination Centaur. The object was discovered on December 18, 2008, by the Siding Spring Survey and measures 79 km in diameter. 2008 YB3 gives a kind of trans-personal visionary and creative intelligence, but one that is rooted in the nurturing of a humane life and emotional reality in contrast to a bombardment of derailed destructive technology. Characteristics: humane versus destructive technology; progressive reactionary with a "back to nature" accent and to stand for this in a gentle way.

The inclination is 105 degrees and the orbital period is 39 years and 259 days. The object remains about 16 years in the sign of Capricorn and much shorter in the other signs, to only about a year in Taurus and Scorpio.

343158 2009 HC82

Love for stormy weather, setbacks due to severe weather and storms, expressions of hydro technology, fluctuating financial pressures and sexual fluctuations.

2009 HC82 is a fairly unique case, because it concerns a retrograde Apollo-asteroid and a NEO (Near Earth Object) with a record speed of 282900 km/h (78.58 km/s) and an inclination of 154.5 degrees. 2009 HC82 measures 1.6 by 3.6 km and was discovered by a team from Catalina Sky Survey on April 29, 2009. The object was at the moment of its discovery in 28 Scorpio conjunct Storm / Rousseau / Amycus, opposition 1996 TL66 / 2001 SQ73 / Mercury in Taurus.

The interpretation of 2009 HC82 in the radix horoscope points to an unusual love for storms and fierce forces of nature, getting a kick out of situations where nature turns out to be stronger than man and civilization and rat race patterns are turned upside down by natural violence; a special energetic and psychological connection with impending storms; benefit from hydrotherapy and a fascination for water locks, water gullies, meanders, mountain streams etc.. There is also a connection between fluctuations in the field of financial and sexual (libido-energetic) pressure. In case of affliction in the first house respiratory disturbances and shortness of breath episodes after exercise or talking can occur, with their cause in a malfunctioning heart pump/blood volume (POTS). In forensic astrology, 2009 HC82 has a link with setbacks caused by storms, expressions of hydro-technology, tornado hunting, storm chasing and hypothetically, when a slow trigger object (e.g. Uranus or Typhon) makes a transit over 2009 HC82 in a nation horoscope, landslides or floods. 2009 HC82 itself transits far too quickly to cause such effects.

The orbital period is 4 years and 73 days.

434620 2005 VD (NAME SUGGESTION PARIAH)

A sudden curse; isolation as a result of a very embarrassing scandal; the fallen idol, falling out of grace; missing out on connection; ultimate test for rediscovering and reclaiming the will to live; Nirguna (important term in Hinduism, meaning: without distinction) experience.

2005 VD is a high inclination retrograde Damocloid of 9.6 km diameter with a very extreme inclination of almost 172.8 degrees. 2005 VD was discovered automatically on November 1, 2005.

Characteristics: the ultimate Fire test where the best of Aries must be claimed and the worst of Leo refused; rejection; isolation as a result of social or societal deformations and getting trapped therein; being caught with a dirty – or not accepted – sex scandal by the general public; a private situation that is suddenly publicly exposed in the media and becomes very embarrassing; being or feeling cursed; missing out on connection, while hyper-conscious of all context and connotation around the origin of the situation in which one finds oneself; becoming a pariah; being completely thrown back on oneself by circumstances; the ultimate test for rediscovering and regaining the will to live. Positively: Nirguna experience; inner invulnerability. Forensic: pariahs; idols falle for scandals; deformations within the Vatican; Kali or Shiva adepts.

Top golfer Tiger Woods, who fell from his pedestal due to a leaked message about his love for pissing over his girlfriend, has 2005 VD in the 5th degree Sagittarius conjunct Piso (*urine, peeing*) / Echeclus / 1999 TD10 / Leviathan; opposition Thereus / Phoinix; square 1996 TO66. 2005 VD was discovered between the 2nd and 3rd degree Aries conjunct the star Deneb Kaitos and heading towards a conjunction with Asbolus with the North nodes in Aries and Black Moons in Leo.

The orbital period is 17 years and 76 days.

471325 2011 KT19 NIKU

Deep reflection and the purging of superficial communication; aversion of the masses and their opinion leader(s), criticizing them; reflection on mass behavior; perceiving the lemming syndrome in others; becoming isolated by one's sideline position; observation of how blind mass behavior creates a negative future; social futurology; feeling/being displaced; unrequited love.

2011 KT19 was nicknamed Niku (rebellious) by the Chinese astronomer Chen. It is a retrograde object (high inclination Centaur) with an orbit almost perpendicular to the ecliptic and an estimated size of about 200 km. Niku was discovered on May 31, 2011, in 2°17 Sagittarius conjunct the fixed star Yed Prior (plus Isidis and Grafias); conjunct the Centaur Chariklo and the asteroids Nymphe and Verdun; square 2007 OR10 / 2003 OP32 in Pisces; square Skuld in Virgo; trine Bacchus / Charybdis / uncorrected Black Moon in Aries; trine 2005 UJ438 in Leo; opposition Ahau / 1996 TL66 in Gemini.

A dominant Niku produces a remarkable personality. Someone who is exceptionally visionary and reflects on the direction in which trends and mass movements or groups are moving and to which discharge or crisis this leads. The result is someone who, on the one hand, condemns the masses and, on the other hand, has a good, loving and human heart because he/she perceives the unconscious obsession-sensitivity of the masses, as well as what directs them towards their obsessions. However, there is an intense aversion to opinion leaders in the Media and all kinds of gurus. Under the skin there is a deep longing for a loving, intense relationship. Niku is a difficult energy to act upon and can easily make a person his own enemy when his viewing ability becomes an obsessor and negative Scorpio-like energy gains momentum.

Characteristics: observation of negative future creation; social futurology; an aversion to, and criticism of, the masses and their opinion leader(s); reflection of mass behavior; the current social-mass psychological "plate tectonics" and a razor-sharp insight in which direction it moves; wanting to put the finger on the sore spot, communicate, write, publish, activate in this sense; becoming isolated in a sideline position; tendency to alcohol abuse rooted in feelings of powerlessness and frustration; dichotomy between the existence and non-existence of a group entity within the masses; learning to separate stigma from group in order to socialize; being forced to relocate because of anti-social pressure from a group culture or annoying trend or mass behavior, or not being able to find a home or settle down somewhere. Interesting in this respect is the horoscope of the New Zealand-born actor Russell Crow, who has lived in Australia since he was four, which he has always experienced as his home country. However, due to a bizarre kink in Australian law, he still did not have Australian nationality at the age of 53. He lost two longer procedures to obtain it, because this constantly keeps giving him a feeling of displacement, that bothers him chronically. In the movie *A Beautiful Mind* he plays a schizophrenic math genius (social sideliner). In *Gladiator*, he pounds straight up against the current (the rebel) of about anyone who comes his way including Emperor Commodus. Russell Crow has Niku conjunct his 4th house cusp (*homeland, home*); trine Pluto (*intense*); sextile Orcus (here: *feeling trapped*).

The orbital period is 212 years and 164 days. Niku spends around 65 years in the sign of Gemini while the 60 degrees of Aquarius and Pisces are transited in only 8 years.

RETROGRADE JUPITER-RESONANT

514107 KA'EPAOKA'AWELA OR BEE-ZED

No surrender, indomitable; the other side of the official version; intrinsic disobedience; imploded power (Vajrayana); courage to stand up against the Molochs, human rights; the outlawed criminal or non-criminal; anarchism that does not reject order but those who exploit it; being unique; awareness of religions as a cover for obtaining crowd obedience.

Ka'epaoka'awela or Bee-Zed is one of the strangest objects in our solar-system. Ka'epaoka'awela is a small asteroid, approximately 3 kilometers in diameter, in a resonant, co-orbital motion with Jupiter. Its orbit is retrograde. Its orbital period is close to the 11.86-year period of Jupiter. During one Jovian year, Jupiter moves 360° around the sun whereas Ka'epaoka'awela moves 366.3° in the opposite direction. Ka'epaoka'awela was discovered on November 26, 2014, by astronomers of the Pan-STARRS survey at Haleakala Observatory on the island of Maui, Hawaii. This unusual object was the first example of an asteroid in a 1:1 resonance with any of the planets. A study has suggested it could be an interstellar asteroid captured 4.5 billion years ago into an orbit around the Sun. The name Ka'epaoka'awela is composed of *ka* 'the', *'epa* 'tricky' or 'mischievous', referring to its contrary orbit, *o* 'of', and *Ka'awela* 'Jupiter'. The name was created by A Hua He Inoa, a Hawaiian-language program dedicated to naming objects discovered with Pan-STARRS (Panoramic Survey Telescope & Rapid Response System).

The discovery-chart of Ka'epaoka'awela shows the object in the 19th degree Leo conjunct Nemesis / Isis / Sila-Nunam in hard opposition to Machiavelli (*political power*) in Aquarius; trine the plutino 2001 KN77 (*anger management*). Nemesis is about unpleasant tidings, guilt issues, shock, disaster. Both Black Moons are in Leo, the corrected Black Moon in the anaretic degree 30 Leo. Uranus in Aries is in exact square with Pluto in Capricorn. Sun is in Sagittarius square Neptune and square Messalina, thus on midpoint Neptune| Messalina and conjunct Vicar. Venus is exactly trine Uranus; Mercury is conjunct Saturn in Scorpio square Nessus in Aquarius and trine Varuna and 2000 OM67. The astrological significance of Ka'epaoka'awela expresses itself via themes as: no surrender, not to be subdued, makes up its own mind; the other side of the official version; loose ends unnoticed by the ruling power; intrinsic disobedience; imploded power (Vajrayana); courage to stand up against the Molochs; human rights, the outlawed criminal or non-criminal; emotional disgust triggered by people who act as dumb system-slaves; does not want to be a part of a machine; anarchism that does not reject order but those who exploit it; attacks the power in charge when ready; being unique, experiencing ones personal individuation as equal to freedom and the true purpose in life; anti-religious, awareness of religions as cloaks for crowd obedience, questioning the power in charge; understanding of the credo "Men are gods who think themselves a man"; a preoccupation with intense eroticism. When the general birth chart indicates a writer, publisher, research journalist or documentary maker, Ka'epaoka'awela can furnish its motivation with years of drafts before quite suddenly publishing something, with a shock effect at exactly the right moment, as some sort of intellectual "sleeping cell", frustrated by the system in power. A peculiar feature can be the mixture of criticism and sex in publications.

The orbital period of Ka'epaoka'awela or Bee-Zed is 11 years and 238 days.

(EX)COMETS

3552 DON QUIXOTE

Fantasy and activism intertwined; eccentric; anachronistic; having a lot of inspiration, but blind spots in communicating ideas.

Don Quixote is an Amor-asteroid and Mars and Jupiter-crosser with still a weak coma, and with this the asteroid holds the middle status between asteroid and comet as a sort of ex-comet. Don Quixote was discovered on September 26, 1983 by Paul Wild. The object measures 18.4 km in diameter and has an inclination of 31 degrees. Don Quixote was named after the foolish knight from the novel of the same name written by Miguel de Cervantes Saavedra, published in 1605; the very first modern novel in our history.

Characteristics: eccentricity; anachronism; having a lot of inspiration, but blind spots in communicating ideas, being misunderstood; learning to see that eccentricity is a form of conservatism if one deliberately acts eccentric because one aspires the image of eccentricity; fantasy that mixes with activism that one has no real grip on; air castles; isolation. In a positive sense a very useful and inspiring object for writers and filmmakers, who move in the zone where fantasy/fiction touches reality. Don Quixote can also parody razor-sharp and thus reveal blind spots, especially the superficial quality of communication – i.e. that of the mass media and politicians – to the man in the street, who takes things too easily for granted.

George W. Bush-advisor and strategist Karl Christian Rove has Don Quixote in Cancer in very close opposition to Mercury / TRIUMF and is known for his so-called "reality making doctrine": All politicians operate within an Orwellian nimbus where words don't mean what they normally mean, but Rovism posits that there is no objective, verifiable reality at all. Reality is what you say it is...

The orbital time of 3552 Don Quixote is 8 years and 263 days.

7968 ELST-PIZARRO

Context; a razor-sharp awareness of context and connotation in everything; hyper-awareness and using it for uttering criticism or offering solutions.

Elst-Pizarro is both a main-belt asteroid and comet (with designation 133P / Elst-Pizarro) and has been discovered twice. On July 24, 1979 as 1979 OW7, by M.R.S. Hawkins, Robert McNaught and Schelte J. Bus, and on July 14, 1996 as 1996 N2 by Eric Walter Elst and Guido Pizarro, after which the object was finally named. Elst-Pizarro measures 3.2 km in diameter.

Characteristics are: context; context and/or connotation as a mirror or lens that defines the (un)soundness of a remark, proposition, conception, process, situation, assumption, habit, status quo, consensus awareness or raising an issue. I do not agree with the – by some astrologers suggested – very negative link of Elst-Pizarro with violence. Rather, there is a strong human element or temperament in Elst-Pizarro that acts as a motivator for spicy criticism. At the most, there could be an emotional outburst based on justifiable indignation linked to this wonderful object.

The orbital time is 5 years and 227 days.

944 HIDALGO

Walking over ice floes; to lose grip and direction and waiting for this "grip" to return in a state of surrender to the situation; situations beyond your control that force you to become assertive.

Hidalgo was discovered by Walter Baade on October 31, 1920, it measures 38 km in diameter and has an inclination of 42.5 degrees. Hidalgo was named after Don Miguel Gregorio Antonio Ignacio Hidalgo-Costilla y Gallaga Mandarte Villaseñor, the priest who led the Mexican War of Independence. It is a fast running Centaur and (almost certainly) an ex-comet. The effect in the chart is very similar to that of Damocles. Hidalgo indicates in the chart where one loses grip on something, the reins must be released and one gets the uneasy feeling of walking over ice floes, while trying to cross the river to the other side in order to reach solid ground again. Conversely, these are pre-eminently phases in which someone gets an enormous incentive to become assertive, being fed up with a situation one doesn't seem to have any grip on. Capricorns in particular will confirm this when their ruler Saturn is hit by a transit of Hidalgo. I have seen many strange interpretations of Hidalgo online, but – on the basis of long empirical research – this is the only interpretation that I can take seriously. Hidalgo is reminiscent of the episode of the TV-series *Jack-Ass* in which several guys take a seat in a shopping cart, descend a hill and just hope it will all end well. Transits to important points temporarily take the control over your life out off your hands, so that you can only rely on your own inner compass.

Dominant in the birth chart (and especially when aspected by Ascendant, Sun, Moon, ruling planet, Almutem Figuris, Midheaven, Pars Fortuna or Black Moon) the energy of Hidalgo demands the necessary attention with regard to balancing the revolutionary impulse with knowledge, good preparation and overview of every important situation and every new trajectory one enters into. The frustrated Hidalgo tends to break out, to take a forced hard stance, or impulsive self-destructive actions. The Hidalgo type should pay more than average attention to assertiveness, strategy, long term planning and tactics, to reap the positive benefits of this Centaur.

The orbital period is 13 years and 281 days.

6144 KONDOJIRO

Dissonance between ones individuality/freedom and the ruling system, not fitting in with the passive herd nor needing to govern them; "humanarchist"; fighting for justice; strong fatalist character; whistle-blower on ethical deformations in the tension zone between the system, authorities, modified reality and the masses ruled by it; becoming a victim of occult forces preying on negative human energy and who defend their food-supply; the Promethean character, role, drama, tragedy.

6144 Kondojiro (1994 EQ3) is an asteroid of about 35 km in diameter. It was discovered on March 14, 1994 by Kin Endate and Kazuro Watanabe at the Kitami Observatory in eastern Hokkaidō, Japan. It is named after Jiro Kondo, a Japanese Egyptologist and professor of archaeology at Waseda University. The orbit of 6144 Kondojiro is unusual for a number of reasons, including:

- An eccentricity greater than 0.3.
- A semi-major axis between that of an outer main-belt asteroid (3.2 AU < a < 4.6 AU) and a Jupiter Trojan (4.6 AU < a < 5.5 AU).
- A relatively low inclination for a Jupiter-crossing minor planet.
- A lack of proper orbital elements due to recurring perturbations by Jupiter.

In the case of such a peculiar orbit it is difficult to classify an object while using a conventional definition. In spite of that, the Minor Planet Center (MPC) lists it as a main-belt asteroid, even though both the orbital and physical properties of 6144 Kondojiro strongly suggest the object is an extinct comet rather than a true asteroid. Apart from astronomical features of an ex-comet, astrologically Kondojiro shows a complexity which is much more typical for an ex-comet than the average main-belt asteroid.

Edward Snowden, who felt fatally trapped between the authorities and the masses – among other aspects contributing to his "public fate" – has Kondojiro at 7 Leo 32'39 minute exact Hylonome (*huge popularity*) at 7 Leo 33'31 square Chaos / Sedna at 7 Taurus 41'59 / 7 Taurus 55'6 (*becoming authentic and isolated*). Julian Assange has Kondojiro in the first degree Gemini opposite Neptune in the first degree Sagittarius (thus strongly aspected on the communication axis) square the "Internet-Cubewano" Albion in the first degree of Pisces.

The orbital period of Kondojiro is 10 years and 132 days

118401 LINEAR

(Re)discovering yourself, becoming who you really are; being straightforward and consistent.

LINEAR is a very different object, because it moves with a normal main-belt asteroid orbit with hardly any inclination, but this object still has a coma and is therefore half a comet and as such indicated with 176P/LINEAR. LINEAR was discovered automatically, by the same **Li**ncoln **N**ear-**E**arth **A**steroid **R**esearch (LINEAR) it was named after, on the day of its discovery on September 7, 1999. The object measures 3.5 km in diameter.

The interpretation relates to straightforwardness, consistency, being consistent, etc. and especially to discovering or rediscovering oneself, getting to know one's true nature and becoming identical to it, in accordance with the Become who you are, which was the motto of the ancient Greek aristocracy. The position and aspects of LINEAR show the themes and processes that are reciprocal throughout one's life and never become really boring.

The orbital period is 5 years and 262 days.

3200 PHAETON

Freeing yourself of things in order to shoot forward, speed, speed mania; flying out of orbit; overestimating your abilities or potential and thus biting off more than you can chew.

Phaeton was discovered on October 11, 1983 by Simon F. Green and John K. Davies and measures 5.10 km in diameter. It is most likely an ex-comet and of all celestial bodies comes closest to the Sun. Phaeton (Ancient Greek: Φαέϑων) is a figure from Greek mythology. Phaeton is a son of the Sun god Helios and his consort Klymene (in some traditions he was the son of Apollo and Klymene). In Greek myth, Phaeton's greatest wish was to drive his father Helios' solar chariot and one day he took his chance. The horses, however, noticed that someone other than their master Helios was holding the reins and ran wild. The solar chariot flew very close to the ground and the heat created large arid areas: the deserts. Afraid that the whole Earth would catch fire, the supreme god Zeus decided to intervene. He threw a lightning bolt at Phaeton, who tumbled out of the chariot and crashed. Phaeton's half-sisters Lampetia and Phaetusa heard of his death and turned their tears into amber and poplars.

Phaeton embodies the urge to free ourselves from all delay, responsibilities, burdens and rules in order to move forward with the substantial risk to strand just before the end goal is reached – usually because of lack of preparation. Phaeton's relationship with speed is evident from the many professional car racers with a strong Phaeton. The positive Pheaton bites the bullit, puts himself at increased speed back on track and keeps the overview. The negative Pheaton is negligent in this area, is only impulsive, ignores all advice, breaks rules, loses its own roots or orientation or crashes down.

Conjunctions with Phaeton give more information about the way one tends to lose grip or where one pulls the brakes out of the fear of losing grip. They show what may run out of control, or where one can take a sprint just after getting the picture complete. Phaeton will be more problematic in Air and Fire and its influence will go over the top faster than in Earth and Water.

The orbital period is 1 year, 158 days and 12 hours.

4015 WILSON-HARINGTON

Future or contemporary oriented, asks out-of-the-box questions; subjecting inert systems or mind-frames to critical in-depth research and/or structural renewal; prophetic insights that materialize later on; Feminism.

Wilson-Harrington is both a periodic comet (107P/Wilson-Harrington) and an Apollo asteroid, which was (re)discovered on November 15, 1979 by Eleanor Helin and named after her predecessors Albert G. Wilson and Robert G. Harrington, who discovered the object on November 19, 1949, after which it was lost again. Wilson-Harrington measures 4 km in diameter.

Its characteristics are: original, out-of-the-box research where criticism and in-depth examination are in synergy. Critical and offensive of old situations, assumptions, systems that only function because of the habitual inertia that maintains them; exposing the inertia of systems or mind-frames, cutting them loose by questioning; truth-finding; authentic thinking; penetrating and exploring the enigmatic; exploring things, situations, subjects; prophetic perceptiveness. Forensic: creators of futuristic theories and conceptions, provoking the boundaries of inert and faulty systems or mindsets that will/could materialize in the future; critics who in the future gain a lot of support and empowerment for their visions and observations; super-detectives. In addition, Wilson-Harrington is often prominent in feminist horoscopes.

The orbital period is 4 years and 104 days.

HELPFUL TIPS

When working with asteroids in addition to the traditional planets and sensitive points and angles, I recommend the use of very small aspect-orbs. In most cases a transit that makes a conjunction or opposition will only be felt between ½° before the minute exact aspect and ½° after. The strongest influence is felt during what we should name the "anaretic arcminutes". Thus at ½° before the minute exact conjunction, during the minute exact conjunction and at ½° (this rule includes even Sedna-Sun conjunctions). Plutinos are an exception as their transits are often already strong at one degree before the aspect is minute exact and dependent on their nature and size, there are also exceptions among objects of other asteroid classes.

You cannot investigate asteroids without either astro-software that includes them or proper online tools. The most useful websites are these:

serennu.com
Number 1 site for your personal asteroid astrology research. I would not have been able to produce this book and my other work on the subject without this superb initiative.

astro.com
I use the "extended chart option" of astro.com in assistance to serennu.com.

astro.com/swisseph/astlist.htm
Complete list of named asteroids.

http://www.true-node.com/eph3/
Very useful for creating an ephemeris.

ssd.jpl.nasa.gov/sbdb.cgi
NASA Jet Propulsion Laboratory asteroid-database.

minorplanetcenter.net/db_search/
Minor Planet Center asteroid-database.

minorplanetcenter.net/iau/lists/NumberedMPs.html
The MPC numbers and discovery dates of all known asteroids so far. If the asteroids received an official name you will find it there. The list starts with number 1: Ceres.

Recommended pioneering asteroid astrology sites:

zanestein.com/Trans-pluto.htm
Zane Stein is one of the most interesting pioneers in asteroid astrology of Centaurs and TNO's.

http://markandrewholmes.com/asteroid.html
Holmes provides a regularly updated list of both main-belt asteroids and other objects including Centaurs, SDOs, Plutinos and Cubewanos.

transneptunian-astrology.blogspot.com
This blog specializes in TNO's and Centaurs, with regular updates.

philipsedgwick.com
Interesting info on TNO's, dwarf planets, Centaurs and more.

vamzzz.com/blog/category/astrology
My own blog-section that deals with astrology, with regular updates.

2020 BOOK RELEASE

Asteroids in Astrology 2: PLUTINOS

Plutinos move through the inner part of the Kuiper belt, which separates the entity of our classic Solar system from the regions beyond. So where the Plutinos orbit, the new encounters the old, the transforming forces clash with the status quo.

Modern astrological research points out that most Plutinos emphasize one or two of the many qualities of their "Godfather" Pluto. They exert a great compelling and penetrating, i.e. plutonic force. They are radical, transforming, confronting and have a Scorpio-like preference for what you might call soul-mining. In other words, they penetrate the depths of the soul, the truth and, like Huya and possibly also Mors-Somnus, even reach into previous incarnations. Negatively they can exacerbate qualities belonging to the darker side of Pluto.

Plutinos expose many crucial missing links, neglected in classic astrology. The chart (and future) of the USA, for example, cannot be understood without implementing these newcomers.

PAPER BOOKS

VAMzzz Publishing creates new and revised editions of books in the categories Magic & Witchcraft, Secret Rites & Societies, Demonology, Celtic & Mythology and Astrology. These books are written by either highly qualified academic researchers, or experts in a special field of esoteric knowledge, craft or practice.

VAMzzz Publishing is a shared passion of Sylvia Carrilho and Benjamin Adamah, located in the heart of old Amsterdam, the Netherlands.

Apart from producing and selling books, we offer each month interesting FREE articles on a wide variety of occult subjects, including folklore and New Astrology. You are welcome to visit our blog: https://www.vamzzz.com/blog

For previews of all our books, please visit our occult bookstore at https://occult-bookstore.vamzzz.com
More books will be added to the list in due time.

www.ingramcontent.com/pod-product-compliance
Lightning Source LLC
Chambersburg PA
CBHW060054070526
44107CB00162B/669